THE CAMBRIDGE MISCELLANY

VIII

REMINISCENCES OF CAMBRIDGE

HENRY GUNNING

Reminiscences of Cambridge

A SELECTION CHOSEN BY
D. A. WINSTANLEY

CAMBRIDGE
AT THE UNIVERSITY PRESS
1932

CAMBRIDGE UNIVERSITY PRESS
Cambridge, New York, Melbourne, Madrid, Cape Town,
Singapore, São Paulo, Delhi, Tokyo, Mexico City

Cambridge University Press
The Edinburgh Building, Cambridge CB2 8RU, UK

Published in the United States of America by Cambridge University Press, New York

www.cambridge.org
Information on this title: www.cambridge.org/9781107628298

First published 1932
First paperback edition 2011

A catalogue record for this publication is available from the British Library

ISBN 978-1-107-62829-8 Paperback

CONTENTS

Introduction

Henry Gunning was born on 13th February, 1768, at Thriplow in Cambridgeshire, and received his early education at Ely and Sleaford. In October, 1784, he entered Christ's College as a Sizar. In the December following he became a Scholar of the College, and in 1788 graduated as fifth Wrangler. In October, 1789, when only twenty-one years old, he was elected Esquire Bedell and held this office until his death sixty-four years later. From the outset of his official career he was distinguished by his conscientious discharge of his duties and by his interest in the forms and ceremonies of the University; and until his eightieth year was a well-known and active figure in academic life. In March, 1847, however, he suffered an accident which permanently crippled him; consequently his health began to fail and for long periods he was condemned to the life of an invalid. In the spring of 1852 he went to Brighton for a fortnight's holiday, hoping to be invigorated by the sea-air; but from that holiday he never returned. Shortly after arriving at Brighton he fell seriously ill both in mind and body, and, after many months of physical suffering and mental distress, died on 4th January, 1854.

It was a sad ending to a pleasant and meritorious life. Gunning, indeed, played his part upon a petty stage and in a trivial drama, but he played it well. He was certainly a very loyal and devoted servant of his University and was probably well content with his modest sphere of activity. Yet he was something more than a painstaking official. He achieved a considerable reputation in his own circle as an amusing talker and raconteur. After his death he was described by a writer in the *Athenæum* as "a cheerful, and, without excess, a convivial man whose company and anecdotes were always welcome"[1]; and such tributes were not always reserved until Gunning was no longer alive to enjoy them. In 1852 Dr Graham, then Bishop of Chester, who had been the Master of a Cambridge college, assured him in a letter that one of the happiest of his Cambridge recollections was "the memory of our agreeable intercourse during each of the years when I held the office of Vice-Chancellor. I well recall to mind how often in our official hospitalities the social hour was enlivened by the flow of your cheerful conversation and the variety of your interesting anecdotes"[2]. But Gunning was liked quite as much for himself as for his stories. Professor Adam Sedgwick, after knowing him for nearly half a century, described him as a most valued friend[3]: and there must have been many who had

---

[1] *Athenæum*, 1854, p. 1038.
[2] *Gentleman's Magazine*, 1854, Part I, p. 207.
[3] *Ibid.*

a very warm corner in their hearts for the pleasant and genial old man. Nor was this affection bestowed upon one who sought at all cost to please. Gunning was a man of strong opinions, especially in politics, and was not deterred from expressing them by the fear of incurring unpopularity. According to his own account he became, when only twelve years old, an ardent adherent of the cause of parliamentary reform, and remained true to his faith even when, in consequence of the fear engendered by the French Revolution, a parliamentary reformer was commonly regarded as an ill-disguised Jacobin. Though he always disclaimed being either an agitator or a propagandist, he boasts that he made no secret of his unpopular opinions and that he suffered for his courage. He never seems, however, to have incurred the extreme penalty of social ostracism. The author of his obituary notice in the *Gentleman's Magazine* records that "though of very decided principles, and not slow in expressing his opinions with warmth and earnestness, it is gratifying to add that Mr Gunning enjoyed the friendship of many excellent persons, whose sentiments differed very widely from his own".

The affairs of the University and not politics were, however, his main interest, and early in his career as Esquire Bedell he began to make notes for a volume of Cambridge reminiscences. He had collected a good deal of material when, about middle life, he suddenly fell dangerously ill; and, realising that he might not survive, became panic-stricken at the thought of the combustible matter he was leaving behind him. "At that period", he wrote, many years later, "many persons were living whose reputation might, perhaps, have been seriously affected by the publication of my anecdotes. I began to reflect whether I had exercised due care in selecting them; I was also apprehensive that I might have inserted some things (which I believed at the time to be facts) upon questionable authority. I had no friend near me on whose judgment I could sufficiently rely, who, after having examined them, would exercise a sound discretion in admitting or rejecting. I feared that these papers might fall into the hands of some bookseller whose only object would be gain....Too ill to admit of delay, I decided on committing all my papers to the flames."[1]

Many years later he was to have cause bitterly to regret this hasty action. In the winter of 1848–9, when he had already become more or less of a chronic invalid, a friend suggested that he might pleasantly employ his enforced leisure in writing his reminiscences. Though over eighty and compelled to rely almost exclusively upon his memory,

---

[1] *Reminiscences of the University, Town and County of Cambridge from the year* 1780, by Henry Gunning (2nd Edition), Vol. I, p. 140.

he determined to attempt the task and set to work seriously in the spring of 1849. It was a bold undertaking for an octogenarian in failing health, and, as he was unable to write much himself, it is probable that he would have made little headway if he had been left entirely unaided. He was fortunate enough, however, to discover a friend, Miss Mary Beart, who was willing to act as his amanuensis; and by the spring of 1852 he had made sufficient progress to contemplate publication in the near future. He issued a prospectus and appealed for subscriptions, but fate intervened in the form of the illness which overtook him at Brighton, and he died with his task unfinished. The *Reminiscences* leave off abruptly at the year 1830, and the work of preparing them for publication and seeing them through the press was undertaken by Miss Beart at Gunning's special request. He naturally chose her as being conversant with his wishes and most anxious to execute them faithfully, and for her the task was a labour of love. There is no doubt, however, that it was a labour. "My occupation", she writes in April, 1854, "has detained me at Cambridge many weeks longer than I at first contemplated. I have been very desirous, in the arrangement, to give as few opportunities, as circumstances will admit, for the comments of the critical reader. To avoid errors I feel to be impracticable; for the most puzzling part of my work has been the arrangement of dates, as dear Mr Gunning was (by his own confession) a very desultory writer, but the marvel will be to many who peruse the work how (at so advanced an age) he would write with *so much vigour*. The memoirs are particularly interesting, and the many anecdotes told in so graphic a style that they cannot fail to amuse; and my solitude has been sometimes enlivened by the enjoyment of a hearty laugh."[1]

Many subsequent generations have laughed with Miss Beart and re-echoed her admiration. The *Reminiscences* are unrivalled as a picture of the University of Cambridge in the last years of the eighteenth and the early years of the nineteenth century; and their conspicuous merit is their liveliness. Gunning had not only a tenacious memory but also a very keen eye for the foibles and weaknesses of his fellow-creatures; and he is certainly at his best when describing the curious and sometimes rather unedifying characters of the Cambridge of his day. In justification for his disinterment of scandal long since dead and buried he urged the importance of registering the advance which had been made in manners and behaviour since the days of his youth; but one may be forgiven for thinking that he was as anxious to adorn a tale as to point a moral. His social experience must have con-

---

[1] *Gunning's Last Years*, edited by A. T. Bartholomew (1912), p. 23.

vinced him of the difficulty of being both charitable and entertaining; and he significantly remarked to Miss Beart that, if she were writing memoirs, she would fall into the error of introducing no character that was not a paragon of virtue and, consequently, bore her readers[1]. Yet, though he certainly cannot be charged with making this mistake, a reviewer was able to say that "with the single exception of Mr Beverley...he speaks forbearingly, if not kindly, of everybody, and seems glad to give them credit for all the good qualities they possessed"[2]. This is on the whole a just remark. Generally speaking, and despite his declared intention of shaming his generation, Gunning is content with making his characters more figures of fun than monsters of iniquity. He is not fundamentally malicious, and is content to show his victims as easy-going men who made light of their responsibilities and were singularly unrestrained by restrictive prejudices.

As he was known to have an eye for the frailties of human nature it is not surprising that the Cambridge dovecot was a little fluttered when it became known that the sprightly Henry Gunning was engaged upon his reminiscences. Though we hear that he received many encouraging letters, it seems that in certain quarters something like

---

[1] *Ibid.* p. 24.
[2] *Athenæum*, 1854, p. 1038,

consternation prevailed. Miss Beart indignantly laments that "there are persons who upon *suspicion* decry the publication"[1], and waxes particularly indignant because, with the exception of the Master of Caius, the Heads of Houses were not subscribers, "although each received a prospectus of the intended publication"[2]. There was, however, no real occasion for alarm. When the *Reminiscences* appeared they were found to deal largely with a long bygone age. Barely more than a quarter of the whole is concerned with the nineteenth century, and the scandals related are mostly drawn from a past which had become a picturesque memory. The Rev. James Backhouse and his associates in the Trinity Seniority were no longer alive to blush for their infirmities.

Expectations, however, were disappointed, as well as fears allayed, by the appearance of the *Reminiscences*. They were found to be not quite so amusing as had been hoped. A reviewer gently complained that the author had hardly lived up to his social reputation, and that he might with advantage have abstained from entering so minutely into the details of University business and forgotten academic controversies. It would be idle to deny the force of this criticism. Gunning is undoubtedly lively but by no means consistently so.

[1] *Gunning's Last Years*, p. 24.
[2] *Ibid.* p. 3.

He includes much which might well have been
omitted and at times degenerates into a chronicler
of unimportant events. Had he lived to revise his
manuscript for the press, he might possibly have
curtailed it; and it is perhaps unfortunate that his
editor, Miss Beart, was so enthusiastic and so
conscientious. There is therefore no necessity to
defend the principle of making a selection from the
Reminiscences; but apologies are certainly required for the selection here presented as much
of value and interest has been omitted. It can
only be pleaded that lack of space and not a
misguided sense of propriety has dictated the
omissions. Students of Gunning, who happen to
glance at these extracts, will certainly miss many
favourite passages; but this little volume is not
intended for them but for the many to whom
Gunning is only a name and often not even that.
Its purpose will have been fully attained if it leads
its readers to make themselves more fully acquainted with a work which of late years has fallen
into undeserved neglect.

These selections have been taken from the
second edition of the *Reminiscences*, in which
certain errors in the first edition were corrected.
The page references in the margins are to the
second edition. A very few notes have been
added where thought to be indispensable, and
these are distinguished from the original notes,

which are asterisked, by being numbered. But anything like systematic annotation did not seem appropriate; and beyond correcting one or two very obvious printer's errors and endeavouring to establish some sort of uniformity in the use of capitals, the text of the second edition has been left unchanged.

Section i

EARLY YEARS AT CAMBRIDGE

A FOX-HUNTING PARSON OF GOOD FAMILY in this county was in the habit of expressing his
contempt for the *canaille*, by saying, "That fellow
never had a grandfather!" I am not one of those
who lay much stress upon ancestry, thinking that
Avos et proavos vix ea nostra voco.

My grandfather was a Fellow of St John's College, and subsequently Precentor and Prælector
Theologicus of Ely Cathedral. He died in 1763,
leaving two sons, both Fellows of St John's, of
whom my father was the younger. But I am desirous to go back a step further, and claim relationship with that most excellent prelate, Bishop
Gunning, who left to the Church all he received
from it, dividing among his relations his savings
from a small paternal estate, which is now in possession of the Rev. William Gunning, Archdeacon
of Bath.

Many of my readers will probably have seen the
monument of the good old Bishop in Ely Cathedral,
and will agree with me in thinking that his epitaph
is his best eulogy. Another undying memorial, also,
remains in that beautiful Prayer for "All Sorts and
Conditions of Men", of which he was the composer.

Vol. I, pp. 1–47

There is also a monument in Ely Cathedral to the memory of James Bentham, the renowned historian, whose fame is too well known to require comment from me. I could never pass this monument in after life without associating the remembrance of his excellent brother Jeffery, who was one of the Minor Canons for nearly fifty years, and a schoolmaster of great repute in that city. His manners were simple and unaffected; he was much beloved by his pupils (of whom I was one); and he contrived so skilfully to combine amusement with instruction, that nothing seemed to us a task. Our play-ground was very extensive; we had the range of the whole College. In bad weather, we sheltered ourselves in the Cathedral; and, incredible as it may seem, we spun our tops and trundled our hoops without interruption. These practices have long since been abolished; and my friend the Dean, with that taste and liberality for which he has always been so justly distinguished, has devoted his time and money to the restoration of that noble structure. May it please God to spare him to see the completion of his great work—a work done with the same spirit as that with which the original pile was raised by its first founders, with whose names his own must for ever remain so justly associated!

It was with much regret I left Ely, as the state of health of our good master obliged him to discontinue his school. I was then sent to the Rev. Edward Waterson, of St John's; and when the Earl of Bristol presented him to the living of Sleaford, in Lincolnshire, with the endowed school there, I followed him, and remained his pupil until I came to college.

I can well remember, when my father came to see me for a few days, his going to the Quarter Sessions, where he was both surprised and pleased to recognise his old college friend, Sir Francis Whichcote, sitting as chairman: they renewed their acquaintance, and my father willingly agreed to spend a day and night at Aswarby. In the morning, the Baronet drove over for him; and after spending a most agreeable day, they smoked their pipes together in the evening, and talked over their college adventures. Sir Francis pressed my father very earnestly to remain a week with him; and to his reply, that he had three churches awaiting him the following Sunday, Sir Francis said he would send a guinea to the churchwardens of each parish, to be laid out as they thought proper, which sum, he remarked, would be a satisfactory excuse for the absence of the parson, unless Cambridgeshire differed very much from Lincolnshire.

That at this period the power of a magistrate was very great, and exercised with very little scruple, the following anecdote will prove:

As Sir Francis was dressing next morning, he perceived the under-groom making very free with his wall fruit. When breakfast was finished, he wrote a note addressed to the keeper of the House of Correction at Folkingham, which he ordered the culprit to take without delay. The note contained the following words: "Give the bearer a dozen lashes; he will guess the reason". This he signed with his initials. Whether the offender was conscience-smitten, or, what is still more probable, took advantage of the wet wafer to acquaint himself with the contents, I know not; but he bribed a helper in the stable, by the promise of a pot of beer and the loan of a horse, to take it for him. The governor, after reading the note, ordered the bearer to be tied up, and the directions were scrupulously obeyed, to the infinite surprise and consternation of the poor fellow, who had no idea of why he was thus treated until his return, when his account of what had taken place caused much merriment in the stable-yard. The tale very soon came to the ears of the Baronet, who laughed very heartily, and took no other notice of it than fining the delinquent half-a-crown for the privilege of being flogged by deputy, and ordered it to be given to the suffering party.

It was my father's intention to have me admitted at St John's; but my county was at that time filled by the Bishop of Ely's Fellow, named Hitch, and

Zachary Brooke (son of the Margaret Professor of Divinity), was already admitted.

After some deliberation, my father decided upon entering me a Sizar at Christ's College, under Parkinson and Seale, at that time Tutors: with the former he was well acquainted. There, also, my county was filled[1]; but the occupant was the Senior Fellow, the Rev. Adam Wall, consequently a vacancy might be expected at no very distant period. The number of admissions at Christ's in my year was only three; two of the men professed not to read, and I was ignorant of the first proposition in Euclid. There had been a contest for the Mastership in 1780, when Mr Barker was elected in opposition to Mr Parkinson. The disappointment of the latter was very great, as he was engaged to a Miss Charlotte Bridge, the most beautiful woman of the day. She was the daughter of a barrister residing on his own property at Harston, in this county. She had lost her mother some years; and her father died soon after her engagement to Parkinson, leaving a son who inherited the estate, and three daughters, who came into a fortune of 1500 *l.* each. When I came to college, Miss Charlotte

October 1784

---

[1] The statutes then in force at several of the colleges did not allow the election of more than two Fellows from the same county. The statutes of Christ's College were still more restrictive, expressly providing, with regard to the twelve Foundation Fellowships, that there should not be two natives of the same county Fellows at the same time.

Bridge was residing with a clergyman's widow at Kennet, in Suffolk; and, though distant from Cambridge at least eighteen miles, Parkinson generally went over three times a-week.

We were lectured immediately after chapel, and generally in a very hasty manner, as Parkinson not unfrequently was equipped in boots and spurs, which his gown but ill concealed, and his servant was waiting with his horse ready to take him into Suffolk. We were usually dismissed with a recommendation to be better prepared for the next lecture. Addressing me particularly one morning, he said, "When you meet with any difficulty, come to me, and I will explain it". It was not long before a difficulty occurred, and I applied for his assistance. He received me very kindly, but I fear he found me incorrigibly stupid; for, after two or three ineffectual attempts to remove the difficulties that puzzled me, he generally added, in a peevish tone, "I cannot make it any plainer, Sir; it requires only common sense to understand it". Disheartened by the difficulties I met with, and annoyed at his contemptuous mode of treating my applications, I determined to give up reading altogether.

Finding this to be the case—for I frankly told him of my intention—he released me from attending his lectures the remainder of the term, remarking that I could doubtless pass my time more

pleasantly, and perhaps more profitably, in my
own room. The occasional outbreaks of impatience
and ill-humour which Parkinson manifested, when
applied to by his pupils to solve difficulties that
came in their way, were very foreign to his natural
character; and were I to say nothing further, I
should have given a very unfavourable, and at the
same time a very unfair impression of him, for he
was, in truth, one of the most kind-hearted and
benevolent men breathing; and in spite of his occasional peevishness, I believe him to have been
much interested for all his pupils, and more especially for myself, for it was in consequence of his
advice that my father sent me to Christ's College.
His natural temper was much changed by the
peculiarity of his situation. The lady, to whom he
had been engaged several years, was much younger
than himself; she was a person of surpassing beauty,
and attracted general admiration wherever she
went. She was not only considered the *belle* of
Cambridgeshire, but at the Bury balls, which were
at that time particularly noted for the assemblage
of rank, fashion, and beauty, she had rarely a rival.
At Bath, which place she occasionally visited, she
was much sought; and having the reputation of
being an excellent horsewoman, wherever she rode,
the gay and fashionable were sure to follow. Parkinson had fully expected to obtain the Mastership
of Christ's in 1780, in which case their marriage

would very soon have taken place. The disappointment was severely felt by both parties. The prospect of a living worth accepting was very remote, and when obtained, the comforts of a rectory house would have been, in the lady's estimation, very far inferior to what she had anticipated in the splendour of a college Lodge. She had refused several offers of marriage during her engagement, and these facts were supposed not to have been unfrequently alluded to by her in terms vexatious to Parkinson. Certain it is that an estrangement eventually took place; and, in the course of a few months, she married Mr Wilshire, an Oxonian, whose father was the wealthy proprietor of a waggon establishment at Bath.

In addition to the severe mental disquiet Parkinson was undergoing, in consequence of his unfortunate engagement, he had involved himself in pecuniary difficulties, principally on the lady's account. The expense attendant on her having two horses and a groom was doubtless defrayed by him, her own income being very limited. He also owed a large sum to the college cook, who, being about to resign his situation, became urgent for payment.

Under all these circumstances, many allowances might have been made for Parkinson's occasional hastiness of temper, for there were times when he seemed quite conscious of it himself. Meeting me accidentally, after I had expressed somewhat ab-

ruptly my determination not to read, he asked me
to breakfast with him. He conversed in the most
kind and friendly manner respecting my future
proceedings, and urged me very earnestly not to
lead an idle life in college; he spoke of the disappointment of my friends, and my own regret when
I reflected that I had wasted the most valuable
years of my life, and lost opportunities never to be
recovered. He assured me that the difficulties of
which I complained were *not insurmountable*, and
that the elements of every science were difficult and
disagreeable. He entreated me, in the most im-
pressive manner, not to throw away the Christmas
vacation, and concluded by renewing his offers of
assistance. There was something so friendly and
even affectionate in his advice and expostulations,
that I felt heartily ashamed of my past conduct,
and resolved on future amendment. I stammered
out my thanks, and we parted on the best terms.

Returning from Parkinson's room in this frame
of mind, I had the good fortune to meet with Mr
Hartley. Hartley was a Yorkshireman, one year
my senior in college; he was an excellent classic,
a hard reading man, and of irreproachable character. He took the degree of sixth Wrangler in
Littledale's year, but did not get either of the
classical medals, for which he was a candidate:
these were obtained by Jonathan Raine, of Trinity,
and Clement Chevallier, of Pembroke.

Hartley and I dined at the same table; but as our pursuits were very different, we were, at the time to which I am alluding, only on speaking terms. The conversation I had held with Parkinson had in two hours effected a complete change in me. I no longer considered Hartley a "*confounded quiz*", a name which the idle and the profligate were in the habit of applying to one of the most respectable of the undergraduates; but I began to look upon him as—in fact he was—one of the most meritorious men in our Society.

When, upon this occasion, we came in contact, I did not return his salutation in the distant manner I had accustomed myself to, but met him with much cordiality. We entered into conversation, and agreed to walk together until dinner-time. He comforted me by the assurance that, at the rate Parkinson travelled over his lectures, it was impossible for any one, not previously acquainted with the subject, to understand or to keep up with him. We spent the evening together, and he convinced me that the difficulties which disheartened me generally arose from not comprehending thoroughly the preceding proposition. He urged me to resume my reading, and to call on him as often as I required his assistance. This offer was made so heartily, and pressed upon me with so much earnestness, that I accepted it without hesitation.

Hartley was in possession of a Tancred student-ship, which, according to the regulation of those days, obliged him to reside eight months in the year, even after he had taken the degree of Bachelor of Arts. In consequence of this, he passed the Christmas and Easter vacations in college*. This residence I might have turned to good account, had I followed his advice and re-mained also; but I could not prevail on myself to be absent from the family reunion at Christmas. I had never passed that season away from the vicarage, and I should have been wretched at being separated from my family during the continuance of that festival.

On those days of my early life, my memory still loves to dwell. It is impossible for any one who has not witnessed it to form an idea of the mirth and hilarity that prevailed at that season. The sports commenced on Christmas-eve, and continued until Twelfth-day, concluding with a very joyous evening. Of these festivities the humblest of the villagers were enabled, either by their own provi-dence, or by the bounty of their more wealthy neighbours, to partake. The children of the poor were taught to sing hymns and carols appropriate

* This absurd custom no longer exists; and a Tancred student, who has taken the degree of B.A., enjoys the emolu-ments of his exhibition until he has taken his M.A. degree, without being compelled to reside.

to the season; and went round the village, for
several evenings preceding Christmas-day, to sing
them before the houses of the inhabitants, and
never failed to return home well furnished with
provisions of a better kind than their own stores
afforded, or with money to purchase them. My
foster-mother, to whom all of us had been sent in
turn, always dined with us on Christmas-day. The
good old woman (whom we dearly loved) always
brought with her a jug of her richest cream, and a
basket of her choicest apples. She joined heartily
in all our sports; but her greatest gratification was
to hear me read a chapter in the Bible, always
selecting the 37th chapter of Ezekiel, which she
never failed to request me to read a second time before she took her departure. She was delighted to
have lived to see her prediction verified, that one
whom she had taught his letters should "turn out
so great a scholar", of which she considered the
being able to read a chapter in the Bible without
hesitation furnished abundant proof. One thing
only was wanting to make her perfectly happy,
and that was, to have seen her "dear child" in his
cap and gown. She had resided more than sixty
years within eight miles of Cambridge, but had
never visited the place. She died the following
spring, after a very short illness. The class of females
to which she belonged exists no longer. I loved her
when living, and, at a distance of nearly seventy

years, I think with respect and affection of Mary Hutchinson.

During the latter end of the October term, as I was going out of college, about seven in the evening, two men on horseback rode into the college shouting most vociferously. I turned back, to see how this unusual occurrence was to end. They galloped once round the court, and then rode off, laughing heartily at the exploit. I heard no more of them that evening, but learned the next morning that the cavaliers made a similar attempt at Sidney College, where the porter shut the gates, and they were taken prisoners. They had begun at Emmanuel previously to my seeing them; and it was said they had betted they would ride round the courts in a certain number of colleges, between the hours of seven and nine. One of them was a Master of Arts, and a Yorkshire Fellow of Catharine Hall, whose name was Clapham; and the other was an undergraduate of Trinity, whose name I do not recollect. I never heard that they were censured in any way; it was looked upon as a very harmless frolic, for which the loss of their bet was a sufficient punishment. Clapham was generally known by the name of Captain Clapham, having once had the command of a provincial corps. He wore, in the afternoon, an enormous cocked hat; and his whole appearance and demeanour were very military. I remember his passing by one evening, when I was walking with Dr Glynn, in front of the New Building of King's, who asked me the name of that "d—d gentlemanly unacademical-looking fellow?"

1785   On the 20th of January I returned to college, and, as it was not usual to begin lectures until after the division of term, I had abundant time to perfect myself in the first six books of Euclid. I made also considerable progress in algebra. Maclaurin was at that time our only text-book; but Hartley furnished me with a manuscript, which proved an excellent commentary, and abounded with examples in which Maclaurin was very deficient. As Hartley and I were the only undergraduates in college, I had no temptation to be idle; and I can reflect on the way I passed these four or five weeks with unmixed satisfaction. The day before our lectures were to begin, Parkinson invited me to breakfast, and I underwent a pretty strict examination in Euclid and algebra. At the conclusion, he complimented me very highly on the readiness with which I applied general principles to particular examples. I felt humbled by "praise undeserved", and confessed to him that I was indebted to Hartley for all I knew; that from him I had derived all the advantage I could have received from a private tutor, and much more, as the latter would have considered that his duty ended with the hour, but that Hartley encouraged me to call as often as I pleased. I might have added, that he never told me that it required nothing but "common sense" to understand the thing that puzzled me. Parkinson said that, under these circumstances, he would dispense with my attendance at lectures, but that he should expect me to call on him once a-week, when he would examine me; at the same time he pointed out a course of reading, which he recommended me to adhere to. I was particularly struck with a remark he made, on my observing that some people supposed Vickers of Queens' would run Brinkley hard for the Senior Wranglership, as he read twelve or fourteen hours daily. "If he mean to beat him", he said, "he had better devote six hours to reading, and six hours to reflecting on what he has read." After more than sixty years' experience, I pronounce the remark to be invaluable.

The Junior Tutor was the Rev. John Barlow Seale, who had been seventh Wrangler and second medallist in 1774, and Moderator in 1779. He lectured in Classics, Moral Philosophy, and Logic. There were assembled at his lectures men of different years, so that we generally mustered a dozen or more. I never missed, as they were to me very interesting, except when he lectured on the Metre of the Greek Choruses, of which I knew nothing, but on which he had (unfortunately for me) published a book. He was a man of very strong prejudices, and accustomed himself, when he wanted to illustrate his subject by an example, to introduce the name of some man who was obnoxious to him. He particularly disliked the Master of his own college; and when speaking of the force of habit, he cautioned us against acquiring bad habits, and generally added, "for want of observing this rule, our *Warden* indulges himself in the most filthy and disgusting of all habits, that of chewing tobacco, which renders him unfit for decent society". Such language was not particularly well calculated to increase the reverence of undergraduates for the Master of their college. This mode of illustrating a lecture was not altogether confined to Christ's College. A friend of mine, of Catharine Hall, related to me a somewhat similar instance that took place in their lecture-room, a few years previously to the time of which I have been speaking. The Tutor, *Cardinal* Thorp (for so he was always called), was lecturing on the law of Extreme Necessity, which justified a man in disregarding the life of another in order to ensure his own safety. He said, "Suppose Lowther Yates and I were struggling in the water for a plank which would not hold two, and that he got possession of it, I should be justified in knocking him off"; and he then added, with great vehemence, "D—n him—and I would do it too, without the slightest hesitation!" It is scarcely necessary to add, that the Tutor had an inveterate dislike to the Master of his college.

Nothing could be pleasanter than the hour passed at Seale's lectures—such was his kindness to all, particularly to those who wished to profit by them. When any ludicrous blunder occurred (which was not unfrequently the case), he joined in the laugh as heartily as any of us. One of his pupils, when construing a passage in Grotius, made a mistake, which set us all in a roar of laughter: the passage was this, "Merite suspecta merx est, quæ hâc lege obtruditur, ne inspici posset". The nature of the blunder will be understood by Seale's remark upon it: "I think, Sir, you have mistaken *merx* for *meretrix*".

Upon another occasion, when he was examining his pupils on a lecture of Locke, which he had delivered the day before, he asked one of them to define "a mixed mode". The man applied to jogged his neighbour to give him an opportunity of reading from his notes. He immediately opened his book, which contained notes on a *chemical* lecture he had been attending the previous day. To the surprise and amusement of his auditors, the pupil, whilst glancing his eye over his neighbour's book, delivered the following answer with great apparent satisfaction to himself, "It is the hardest of all metals, malleable, fusible, and soluble in aqua regia".

Parkinson was at this time publishing a formidable quarto on Mechanics (the work was never

popular, and is now almost forgotten). He sent me
several sheets in manuscript; I worked at them
very hard, and made myself master of that part of
it which treated on elastic balls, and was able to
investigate the centres of oscillation, gyration, and
percussion (as taught in his book), very much to
his satisfaction.

When Porteous, whom Seale was in the habit of
calling the Queen's Bishop, was promoted to the
see of London, Seale confidently expected to be
appointed his chaplain. To the surprise of the
college, and to the infinite mortification of Seale,
Ormerod, whose talents and acquirements Seale
held in supreme contempt, and whom he had
nicknamed the "Queen's Bishop's Pawn", was
selected to fill the situation. It was upon this occasion that Fawcett of St John's exclaimed, when
Seale entered the Masters of Arts' reading-room,
"Have you heard that the Queen's Bishop's Pawn
has got a move?" This ironical allusion to Seale's
favourite game raised a hearty laugh among the
M.A.'s, in which Seale could not participate. It was,
however, not long before it was his turn to laugh,
for he was soon after appointed chaplain to the
Archbishop of Canterbury. This appointment did
not prove so agreeable as he expected: from an unfortunate peculiarity of temper, he never stayed a
week at a friend's house without disputing with
some of the servants. At Lambeth, he took a particu-

lar dislike to the Archbishop's butler, which was considerably increased, when, on the occasion of Dr Parr dining *tête-à-tête* with him one day, Seale ordered a second bottle of sherry, when the butler replied, "he had already furnished as much sherry as was allowed at the chaplain's table". The frequent complaints to the Archbishop of the conduct of his servants, interrupted that harmony which had previously subsisted between them; and his Grace availed himself of an early opportunity of offering Seale the living of Stisted, in Essex, which became vacant about that time, and which was most gladly accepted. Seale returned to college, and was considered by the Society to be in his year of grace; but an unexpected decision of the Visitor enabled him to hold this living with his fellowship. He finally took the living of Anstey, which, with Stisted, he held till his death. He associated very little with the clergy or gentry in the neighbourhood of his preferments, but passed a good deal of his time in inferior society. The latter part of his life was very unsuitable to a man of his talent and acquirements. He had filled with great credit the situation of Tutor, and deputy Professor of Divinity, and might (had he been a man of sound discretion) have risen to the highest offices in the Church.

The University began to fill again, and my reading was interrupted by repeated invitations to supper. The host observed, as we came out of chapel, "We intend to have a rubber". This was an invitation I could never withstand, and it was only mischievous in this respect, that it occupied the time from half-past six till nine, which I found best adapted for study. Short whist had no existence at that time; we played shilling points, and occasionally half-a-crown was betted on the rubber. Gambling was not the vice of the University. There were a few men amongst the Masters of Arts of pretty high standing, who cultivated the acquaintance of the young nobility, and contrived to keep a handsome establishment, and live in a very expensive style, without any other apparent resources than their fellowships. Two of the most celebrated (I was very near using the word notorious) were Akehurst and Pulteney, both Fellows of King's. At a dinner given by the Bishop of Llandaff to the Duke of Rutland and some other young men of high rank, the Bishop was pressed by Akehurst to take a seat at a table where there was a vacancy, and at which they had been playing for very high stakes. This was the very significant answer of the Bishop—"I have no estate to lose, Sir; I am not desirous of winning one".

My most intimate friend out of my own college was Joseph Staines Banks, of Trinity Hall, through whom I formed a more extensive acquaintance than was consistent with the plan of reading I had determined on. We had become attached to each other as schoolboys, and when we separated, an uninterrupted correspondence was kept up.

When Banks was an undergraduate, his manners were courteous and gentlemanly in the extreme, and contrasted strongly with the coarser behaviour of his contemporaries. He always carried cards in his pocket, with his name and college written on them, which was considered *over refinement* by the generality of students, who, when they made a call, knocked a piece of mortar out of the wall with the key of their room, and with this scrawled their names on the doors of their friends. Some were refined enough to carry a piece of chalk in their pockets. To his credit be it said, that though Banks visited every man in his college (which was at that time the most riotous in the University), and gave frequent and expensive entertainments, I do not remember ever to have seen him guilty of drunkenness, at that time almost universal. Our intimacy continued without interruption through a long series of years. He died at Hemingford in the autumn of 1848, at the advanced age of eighty-three.

A circumstance took place in the summer of this year, which was productive of much amusement to the younger members of the University.

Dr Kipling, who always preserved *an immeasurable distance* between himself and the undergraduates, was by no means popular among them;

indeed, he mixed but little in any society, his time being much engrossed in a voluminous work he was preparing for the press. His principal relaxation was a daily ride to "*the Hills*", which at that time was the most frequented road amongst the members of the University. Returning one day, he picked up an ostrich feather which he saw drop from the hat of a lady, who was proceeding very slowly about fifty yards in advance.

On overtaking her, he presented the feather, accompanied by an expression relative to his good fortune in being able to restore it. The lady thanked him for his kindness, and expressed her annoyance that her servant was not in attendance—said she had just left General Adeane's, and had no doubt but her groom was following her—but she feared he might have been induced to partake too freely of the well-known hospitality of the servants' hall at Babraham. The Doctor begged her not to be uneasy, as he should have much pleasure in attending her until her servant appeared. They had not proceeded far before they began to meet parties of young men, who were going out for their morning's ride. From the significant glances that were exchanged between these parties and the lady, Dr Kipling could not fail to discover he had got into bad company. That he might rid himself of his new acquaintance as quickly as possible, he clapped spurs to his horse, which had been selected with the well-known Yorkshire discernment. The lady was also well mounted, and applying her whip briskly, kept up with the Doctor. When they entered the town, many familiar faces were encountered, who stared in utter amazement; and when passing *Llandaff House* the horses were neck and neck. Fortunately for the Doctor, his stable was in Emmanuel Lane, and his horse turning sharply round the corner, his companion proceeded on her way. The name of this person was Jemima Watson; she lived in expensive lodgings, where she was in the habit of receiving some of the most fashionable men in the University.

Many a laugh was raised at the expense of the Doctor's credulity in becoming so easy a victim to a previously concerted plan.

At length the arrival of the Commencement (before which few undergraduates were allowed to leave the University) set us free, and I returned to the vicarage. The Commencement, which in these days is the dullest, was at that time the gayest season in the University. A nobleman scarcely ever took his degree except on the Monday in that week; and I recollect that on one occasion, when Dr Pearce was Orator, eleven persons took their degrees in right of nobility[1]. The sermon for the

---

[1] Under the Elizabethan statutes the University was able to admit to any degree Privy Councillors, Bishops, Noblemen and the sons of Noblemen though they had not kept the terms or complied with the forms prescribed for the degree.

benefit of Addenbrooke's Hospital was preached
on the Thursday in the preceding week, and always
secured a crowded church. Some celebrated
singers, who were engaged to attend at the concerts
and oratorios which usually took place about that
time, used to volunteer their services. The gentry
and the clergy, from the most distant parts of the
county and isle, made a point of being present.

The fair on Midsummer Green, known by the
name of "Pot Fair", was in all its glory. There
were booths at which raffles for pictures, china, and
millinery took place every evening, which were not
over until a late hour. The Saturday evening preceding the Commencement brought together the
greatest assemblage of company; the gentry in the
town and neighbourhood, and many persons from
the adjoining counties, used to be present. It was
not unfrequently the case that twenty private carriages were in waiting. The promenade extended
from the place where the fair is now held, to the
grounds of Barnwell Abbey. Amongst the company, groups of Masters of Arts, consisting of four
or five in a party, *who had evidently dined*, were to
be seen linked together arm-in-arm, and compelled
all they met with to turn out of the way. Difficult
of belief as it may be in the present time, amongst
these you might discover many Fellows of colleges,
and not a few clergymen. On that evening the
ladies elected one of the noblemen, who was to take

his degree on the following Monday, to be the steward of the Commencement Ball, which always took place on the evening of that day. During that night, and on the Sunday, couriers were despatched in all directions to the chief families within thirty miles of the place, inviting the ladies of each family to the ball. No lady could come without an invitation, but tickets were sent in great profusion: no charge was made for ladies' tickets, but every gentleman paid a guinea on admission. The entertainment was a very splendid one; and the steward, on paying his bill (which he always did in the course of the week), generally found himself out of pocket; but if upon any occasion there was a surplus, it was given to the Hospital. On Commencement Sunday, the college walks were crowded. Every Doctor in the University wore his scarlet robes during the whole day. All the noblemen appeared in their splendid robes, not only at St Mary's and in the college halls, but also in the public walks. Their robes (which are now uniformly purple) at that time were of various colours, according to the tastes of the wearers— purple, white, green, and rose-colour, were to be seen at the same time*. The people from the neighbouring villages then never ventured to pass the rails which separate the walks from the high road. The evening of Commencement Tuesday, if

* Lord Chartley wore rose-colour.

not the most numerous, was always the most splendid assemblage at Pot Fair, when the merits of the steward and the events of the ball formed the chief subjects of conversation.

When the term ended, the University was far from being deserted. No college was entirely without resident members during the long vacation. At King's and Trinity, a certain number of the Scholars were obliged to reside during the summer; and many Fellows of colleges never slept out of the University for a great number of years together. The last of this class was Mr Burrell, the Bursar of Catharine Hall, who used to take his daily walk in what is called "The Grove", and who never travelled further than the Senate House, except once, during the long vacation, when the Master of the college prevailed upon him to walk half-way to Grantchester.

I passed my first long vacation very unprofitably, my time being chiefly occupied in fishing, shooting, and occasional visiting. I returned to college towards the end of September, and, by the advice of Hartley, I left my gun in the country. I applied very closely to study, and availed myself most fully of the assistance so kindly and so cordially pressed upon me by my friend. He and I, with Mr Adam Wall, the Senior Fellow, were the only residents till the middle of October, when the election of college officers took place, which brought

up several of the Fellows. I had thus six clear
weeks for reading, as lectures did not commence
until after the division of term. As soon as Parkinson came, he asked me to breakfast, when rather a
long examination took place, with which he was
not dissatisfied. During the summer, three or four
persons had migrated from other colleges, so that
there were six or seven undergraduates of my year;
but as the new comers were decidedly non-reading
men, Parkinson resolved that they should attend
lectures with the year below them: he at the same
time recommended that I should continue to profit
by Hartley's kindness, and come to him once a-week
to be examined. I left him with a full determination of following his advice; but the frost set in
early, and, on the arrival of information that an
unusually large flight of snipes had settled in
Bottisham and Wilbraham Fens, I applied to
Henshaw for a gun, and, in company with some
fellows as idle as myself, set off in quest of them.
The term, however, was not wholly passed in
these pursuits; and though I did not call on
Hartley so frequently as he wished, I never failed
to call on Parkinson at the time appointed, and he
was tolerably well satisfied with my progress. On
Christmas-day, our family party assembled as
usual at the vicarage; but the absence of the good
old woman who had nursed us all was so severely
felt that the day passed off heavily, and affected

even my father, whose spirits were of the most buoyant kind.

1786   I returned to college very early in January, and consequently had several weeks for reading before the University filled. I applied myself very closely, and with the assistance of Hartley made considerable progress; so that when Parkinson summoned me, I waited upon him with a well-founded confidence that I should pass the examination to our mutual satisfaction. Hartley was delighted with my account of the interview, and laid down a course of reading which, though I was fully sensible of its advantages, I had not resolution to adhere to. Unfortunately there were several persons in college of the year below me, who were most agreeable, companionable men, but all of them remarkably idle. Basil Montagu, Bob Porteus (nephew of the Bishop of London), George Leapingwell (the father of my colleague)*, Tom Bullen, and Joe Tayler, were my chief associates in college; and if my only object in coming to the University had been to pass my time agreeably, I could not have made a better selection. But I had seasons of bitter reflection; the idea would intrude itself that I had been sent to college for a very different purpose; and after having passed a very delightful day, I was kept awake a great part of the night

* George Leapingwell, Esq., LL.D.

by vexation and remorse. How much more real
happiness had I enjoyed, when Hartley and myself
were almost the only persons in college, than I did
after the arrival of my gay companions, which I
had anticipated with so much pleasure!

But the most mischievous person in the Society
was a Bachelor of Arts, named Tunstal. He was
the nephew of Dr Shepherd, the Plumian Professor,
and had taken his degree in 1784, when he was
senior medallist, George Gordon (afterwards Dean
of Lincoln) being the junior. He was just come to
reside in college, having been since his degree private tutor in three or four different families, all of
which he had left with disgrace. Had his industry
and good conduct borne any proportion to his
talents, he would have been one of the most distinguished men in the University; but he was the
idlest of the idle, and so low a profligate, that even
in those days, when the standard of morals was not
very high, he was shunned by all the men of his
own standing. Deprived of the society of his
equals, he was constantly scheming to introduce
himself to young men who had heard nothing of
his character. I was getting my breakfast, soon
after the Christmas vacation, when he knocked at
my door, and apologising for the intrusion, asked
leave to fill his tea-pot from my kettle, as he had
suffered his fire to go out. I invited him to breakfast with me; he accepted the offer, and fetching

his bread and butter, was in a few minutes perfectly at home. The conversation was very entertaining, and in the course of it he took care to inform me (apparently without design) that he had gained the first medal. He paid me a very long visit, and I confess that I was very proud of my new acquaintance. My bedmaker came in soon after, and made me acquainted with his true character. The old woman said that when he left college he was in every one's debt, and that he had shown himself so utterly devoid of principle, and treated his creditors with such insolence, that he could not obtain a quarter of a pound of tea on credit. In proof of her assertion she looked into his tea-pot, which he had forgotten to take away, and it did not contain a single particle of tea; she then added, that he had played the same trick on almost every one in college who was unacquainted with him. At other times he would beg to remain a few minutes in the room of a stranger, till his bedmaker came to open the door of his own room, which had been inadvertently shut in his absence; but this invariably happened when the stranger had a party drinking wine with him. By these disreputable shifts, he contrived to procure a tolerable share of the comforts which college afforded, equally regardless of the sneers of the younger, and the contempt of the senior members of the Society. It was then the custom for the undergraduates to send in to the Dean once a-week a Latin theme: this he would volunteer to write for any one who complained of the difficulty of the task. He affected to be angry when offered a compensation, but he was not long before he took an opportunity of *borrowing* a much larger sum than he could have ventured to ask for as the price of his labour. He was a tolerable musician, and a very close intimacy took place between him and Tom Bullen, who was passionately fond of music. At that time the grand commemoration of Handel took place in Westminster Abbey, under the direction of Joah Bates. Bullen was most anxious to be present, but despaired of raising the requisite funds. Tunstal told him that was no object, as he was daily expecting to receive a large sum of money: he would defray the whole expense, and Bullen might repay him when it suited his convenience. Preparations were made for their departure, and they only waited for the letter containing Tunstal's remittance. At length it came; it contained no money, but an assurance that in the beginning of the following week he might depend on receiving it. Tunstal affected to treat the disappointment very lightly, but Bullen had set his heart upon going to the Abbey, and was seriously annoyed at the circumstance. At length Tunstal suggested, that if Bullen knew any one in the University who would advance the money for a week, at the end of that time he should be punc-

tually repaid. Bullen said that a Fellow of Sidney,
of the name of Heslop, a particular friend of his
mother, would lend it him for that short time. He
made the application and succeeded, and the two
friends set off for town. They attended several of
the meetings in the Abbey, and at the end of the
week thought of returning to Cambridge. On examining the state of their finances, they found that
they had barely sufficient to take them to Cambridge on the outside of the coach. Tunstal proposed that they should put into their pockets and
wrap about their persons as much of their clothes
and linen as they conveniently could, and that the
rest should be left at the Golden Cross, Charing
Cross. Tunstal's whole wardrobe was disposed
about his person; but Bullen was under the necessity
of leaving a considerable part of his behind, particularly a coat which he had scarcely worn. In
walking towards the George and Blue Boar, Tunstal laughed at his friend for his reluctance at
leaving his best coat behind. A quarrel took place,
and they parted, Tunstal taking the coach for
Cambridge, and Bullen returning to the Golden
Cross. He then confessed to his landlord the trick
he had intended to play him, and told him how he
had been duped by his friend. The landlord was
pleased with his frankness, and suffered him to de-
part the next morning, taking his baggage with
him, a written promise being given by Bullen that

he would send the money that was owing the very first opportunity. When he returned he applied to Tunstal for the money, who told him that his friends had deceived him, and that he was not likely to get any from that quarter. Heslop dunned poor Bullen two or three times a day, and at length applied to his mother, who out of a very limited income sent her son sufficient to pay his debts. In the spring of the following year Tunstal, who had been an unsuccessful candidate for a fellowship, was obliged to quit college: he went to America, where he became an assistant in a school.

Among the persons whom I was in the habit of meeting at the rooms of my friend Banks was Hare Townsend, a Fellow-commoner of Trinity Hall, and the only son of Alderman Townsend, of Bruce Castle. By relating an anecdote concerning him, I can best illustrate the manners of the University at that particular period. Entering the hall of Magdalene College one evening, much intoxicated, when the Society were at supper, he went to the Pensioners' table, laughed at the paltry fare with which they were regaling themselves, and said, if they would sup with him the following evening, he would show them how gentlemen ought to live. The Fellows were at supper at the upper table, but though he was in his cap and gown, and made a great noise, they took no notice whatever of the intrusion. Strange and almost incredible as it may

appear, it is a positive fact that all the members of
the Pensioners' table (with the exception of two or
three) accepted the invitation thus given from a
man they had never seen before. The next evening
the undergraduates went in a body to Townsend's
room; he had ordered a magnificent supper to be
prepared, and desired the butler to buy a new pail
in which the punch was to be served up. As the
butler was carrying the pail across the court in the
dark, a magpie belonging to the college, whose con-
versational talents had rendered him a great
favourite with the whole Society, perched upon
the edge of the pail. The butler attempted to brush
him off, but unfortunately brushed him into it:
this was not discovered until the pail was set upon
the table, when the magpie was irrecoverably dead.
The evening was passed in a convivial manner,
perfectly new to the undergraduates of Magdalene,
whose temperate habits and devotion to tea were
quite proverbial.

I well remember another occurrence at Trinity
Hall, which happened within my own knowledge.
One of the Fellow-commoners had taken his degree,
and was about to quit college, which event they
celebrated in the following manner: After supper,
they brought into the centre of the court all the
hampers they could find filled with straw, on the
top of which they placed his tables, and on these
they set the chairs, and the whole were surmounted

by his cap, gown, and surplice: they then set fire
to the hampers, and with loud shouts danced
round the pile till the whole was consumed. No
college censure was passed upon the actors in this
frantic exhibition, nor was there any investigation
into the circumstances.

The great source of idleness, which consumed
more time than all my other employments put together, was my *passion* for shooting, for which di-
version Cambridge afforded the most extraordinary
facilities. In going over the land now occupied by
Downing-terrace, you generally got five or six
shots at snipes. Crossing the Leys, you entered on
Coe-Fen; this abounded with snipes. Walking
through the osier-bed on the Trumpington side of
the brook, you frequently met with a partridge,
and now and then a pheasant. From thence to the
lower end of Pemberton's garden was one continued
marsh, which afforded plenty of snipes, and in the
month of March a hare or two. If you chose to
keep on by the side of the river, you came to
Harston-Ham, well known to sportsmen; and at no
great distance from this you arrived at Foulmire
Mere, which produced a great variety of wildfowl.
The heavy coach changed horses at the Swan, and
would set you down, between seven and eight
o'clock, at the Blue Boar. If you started from the
other corner of Parker's Piece, you came to
Cherryhinton Fen; from thence to Teversham,

Quy, Bottisham, and Swaffham Fens. In taking this beat, you met with great varieties of wildfowl, bitterns, plovers of every description, ruffs and reeves, and not unfrequently pheasants. If you did not go very near the mansions of the few country gentleman who resided in the neighbourhood, you met with no interruption. You scarcely ever saw the gamekeeper, but met with a great number of young lads, who were on the look-out for sportsmen from the University, whose game they carried, and to whom they furnished long poles, to enable them to leap those very wide ditches which intersected the Fens in every direction. I am happy to say that these incentives to idleness no longer exist. Thousands and tens of thousands of acres of land, which at the time I speak of produced to the owners only turf and sedge, are now bearing most luxuriant crops of corn. By removing a number of locks, which were formerly considered essential to the navigation of the Cam, and by deepening the channel, they have at the same time improved the river, and drained the lands to a considerable distance from its banks. At a few feet below the surface they meet with clay*, which proves the most valuable manure to the land; the crops are most abundant, and in a

* Oak-trees, as black and almost as hard as ebony, together with the antlers of stags, are found in great numbers, from which it appears that the Fens were once a huge forest.

few years the rents will be much higher than those
of the best uplands. A large steam-engine, that
was erected for the purpose of throwing the super-
fluous water into the river, is frequently employed
in throwing it back again to supply the cattle with
water, of which in dry summers they are frequently
in want. The sport which the Fens afforded, and of
which I was so fond, unfortunately could be pur-
sued with success during every month in the year.
A very common practice, during the spring and
summer months, was for a party to divide into two
sets, one on a shooting scheme, and the other on a
boating and fishing expedition, both parties agree-
ing to meet and dine at Clayhithe. There was a
public-house on each side of the river, where fish
was dressed to perfection; the charges were very
moderate, and the ALE very good. The fishing-party
(who frequently went as far as Upware, and occasionally to Dimmock's Court) scarcely ever failed
to get an abundance of fish; but if they were unfortunate, the landlord of the smaller house had
well-stored ponds, from which the deficiency was
quickly and amply supplied. Some of the party
were in the habit of gambling in the following
way: They bargained with the proprietor of these
ponds to be allowed to keep all the fish they caught
at a single throw, or any number of throws, for a
sum agreed on: the sum varied from half-a-crown
to a guinea, according to the size of the net, the

skill of the caster, the state of the ponds, and the number of throws. Two things were remarkable; though some splendid pike and perch were occasionally caught, yet the proprietor was always a winner. Sometimes I have been called out to see a person land an enormous fish which was visibly enclosed in the net. In his anxiety to make sure of his prize, he thankfully followed the advice, or gladly accepted the assistance, of a good-natured bystander, who was smoking his pipe by the side of the water, and who was usually *a friend of the landlord*; it is scarcely necessary to add, that with such an assistant the huge fish generally escaped. The pull against the stream, with the unwieldy boats then in use, was an arduous task, and we returned home more fatigued by our day's *pleasure* than a bricklayer's labourer after the hardest day's work.

Smoking was at that time going out of fashion amongst the junior members of our combination rooms, except on the river in the evening, when every man put a short pipe in his mouth. I took great pains to make myself master of this elegant accomplishment, but I never succeeded, though I used to renew the attempt with a perseverance worthy of a better cause. When we arrived at Chesterton, two or three of our party would sometimes leave the boat and stop to play at billiards; but this was generally disapproved of, and the billiard-players were seldom admitted into our future parties.

At that time supper was the usual meal of society, the cooks (by an order made the year before I came to college) not being allowed to furnish a dinner to an undergraduate without a note from one of the Tutors, which was never granted except some strangers were expected. A supper, to men of your own college, was in general a very harmless, inexpensive affair. At eight o'clock, your bedmaker brought you a "*sizing-bill*" (a bill of fare, in which the price of each article was set down); you chose what you thought proper, and ordered it to be taken to the room of the friend by whom you had been asked to sup. As we dined at half-past one, and there was no supper in the hall, there were several of these parties every night. Our host furnished bread and cheese, butter and beer. No wine was introduced, but the master of the feast prepared, before the arrival of his guests, a quantity of punch which he put into a tea-pot, and placed on the hob by the fireside to keep it hot. These tea-pots were of various sizes (some of them enormous), and supplied by the bed-makers, who charged according to the size. Nothing could be more unexceptionable than these meetings.

One of the places of attraction about this time was a very small and humble looking house, about the middle of what is now called King's Parade, in

which was a shop window fitted with a glass case,
containing trinkets and jewellery of various kinds.
At the back of this case was placed a chair sufficiently elevated to show the bust of the person who
sat on it. As soon as the fashionable world began
to move, which at that period was between 10 and
11 A.M., this seat was occupied by a very handsome
girl, whom it was not a difficult matter to recognise
as a Jewess. The shop, which would not hold more
than half-a-dozen persons, was always filled with
University men, usually among the higher class,
and in the course of the morning a considerable
portion of the contents of the glass case had found
purchasers; some of them were taken away, but the
larger portion were offered to the Lady of the
Shrine which, with much affected reluctance, she
at length consented to receive. These little coquett-
ings displayed by the young Jewess were most
fascinating, and showed she had been skilfully
trained. The trinkets thus restored gradually found
their way again into the glass-case, where they
were so judiciously arranged that few persons
would detect having seen them before. Rose Elkin
was in truth a finished coquette; she was devoted
to admiration, but I never heard the slightest im-
peachment on her character. She was never to be
seen in the street without her mother; and when
any party was formed, or any country excursion
planned, she only accepted the invitation with the

proviso that her mother was to accompany her. I remember but one man who could boast of having had a *tête-à-tête* with her; his name was Dilke, of Emmanuel, and he effected it by the following stratagem: A party had been formed for passing the day at Bourn Bridge, and Dilke was to convey her and her mother. When they arrived at Babraham plantations, he contrived to drop his handkerchief, as if by accident, out of the carriage window. The old woman begged him to pick it up, but he replied he would not leave the carriage for a dozen handkerchiefs. She remonstrated with him on his extravagance, remarking on the texture of the cambric, being of the most expensive description. He laughingly told her, that if she would get out and pick it up, she should have it for her trouble. When fairly on her way, Dilke intimated to the postilion to drive on, and the old lady was obliged to follow on foot to Bourn Bridge, which was, fortunately for her, but a very short distance. She arrived in a great rage, but was at length pacified by Dilke promising her five more handkerchiefs to make up a set.

Some of the aristocratic admirers of the beautiful Jewess (for she was indeed beautiful, and Shylock would have been proud of her, particularly as she would have added to his jewels, instead of squandering them away), were very desirous she should be seen by the Prince of Wales, who never failed attending Newmarket Races.

The Prince at that period surpassed all the nobility as much in personal appearance as he did in rank: although rather inclined to be fat, he was not corpulent. In dress and address none could rival him, and he was already distinguished for the elegance of that bow, of which, at Hastings' trial some years after, Chancellor Thurlow spoke with so much contempt.

Rose Elkin accompanied her mother upon one occasion to Newmarket Races. When the carriage appeared on the ground, it was soon surrounded by the fashionable men of the University. During the morning the Prince approached, when the cavaliers then in attendance fell back. The Prince was introduced by a friend, and conversed with her for a quarter of an hour. Nothing could be more affable and courteous than his demeanour; he took leave of her with great politeness, but never expressed a desire to see her a second time. The fact was, the Jewess was remarkably small and slender, and the Prince even at that early age judged of the beauty of a woman as a Lincolnshire grazier does of the value of an ox, by its propensity to fatten. Rose Elkin left Cambridge for Portsmouth soon after the time I am speaking of; she was ultimately married most respectably to a person of her own persuasion, of the name of Harte.

As soon as the long vacation arrived, I hastened to the vicarage, and passed this summer much as I

had done the preceding one. I returned to college
the beginning of October, and as Hartley was
reading day and night for his exercises in the
schools, I did not feel myself at liberty to apply to
him so often as I had previously done: with this I
acquainted Parkinson, who very kindly had me to
his rooms two hours during each week, and I received much benefit from his advice and instruction.

At Christmas our family party were assembled at
the vicarage, but our pleasure was alloyed in consequence of several of my brothers and sisters having
the ague. It had been my father's constant practice, ever since he had lived in the country, to dine
in the hall of St John's College on St John's Day,
always returning home to dinner the following day.
This year I persuaded him to stop and dine in the
hall of Christ's College on their annual feast, which
was held about that time. An occurrence took place
that evening, which, though a member of a college
more remarkable for its cordial hospitality than for
the refinement of its manners, struck my father
with astonishment. After dinner, the party, which
was very numerous, adjourned to the combination
room. There was a long table reaching from one end
of the room to the other, at the top of which the
Master presided, and at the bottom Parkinson was
seated. The guests and the senior members of the
University having arranged themselves at this

table, twelve or fourteen persons, for whom there
was no room, seated themselves at a smaller one
near the fire. This table, over which Metcalfe, one
of the Senior Fellows, presided, soon became a
thorough nuisance. At the upper table, the Master
gave at intervals the standard toasts, which, according to the rules observed in every well-regu-
lated society, ought to have been repeated by the
president at the lower one; but here each person
was called on in succession to give a sentiment, the
meaning of which was very *equivocal*, or rather,
very *unequivocal*. Amongst the most vociferous of
this party was Busick Harwood, a Bachelor of
Physic of the same college. In about an hour they
became quite uproarious; each toast, which might
be distinctly heard by every person in the room,
was greeted with shouts of applause and rapping on
the table, and the jokes that followed were greeted
by the loudest laughter. Any one passing by the
smaller table was laid hold of, and forcibly detained
until he had purchased his liberty by drinking a
bumper of port. At length Parkinson was requested
by the Master to ring for tea; but not being able
to get at the bell, except by passing within reach of
the smaller table, he was immediately seized, and
required in the most unceremonious way to drink
the bumper that was tendered. This he declined
with more courtesy than his assailants were entitled to, but in a tone the most firm and decided:

still they kept their hold, and the clamour became deafening, several persons exclaiming, "Make him drink it! Force it down!" At length the Master, quitting his seat, interfered on behalf of Parkinson, when comparative peace was restored.

I cannot refrain relating a circumstance which happened in the same room at one of these annual feasts. William Fisher was always invited by his brother the Commissary: he was distinguished for wearing a remarkably handsome cocked hat, and always mounted a new one in honour of the day. Searching for his hat when leaving, he found but one remaining, and that so shabby and dirty, he would not put it on, but left it behind him. The following year he was again played the same trick, the delinquent of the previous year availing himself of another new hat, and leaving the *old one* behind him.

I returned to college the beginning of January, as I was particularly anxious respecting my friend Hartley's degree, the examination for which was to begin on the following Monday. His position on the Tripos disappointed me extremely. Littledale and Frampton were always considered as first and second; but I felt no doubt that my friend would be third, instead of which he was the sixth. To my certain knowledge he had afforded much friendly and gratuitous assistance to the person who occu-

Vol. 1, pp. 72–78. 1787

pied the third place; but Hartley never expressed
the slightest dissatisfaction, but bore it with his
usual equanimity. When I was at breakfast on the
following Monday, the Proctor's man put into my
hand a paper, on which were written these *tremen-
dous words:*

> Gunning, Coll. Christ., Resp. 5to die Februarii.
>   T. JONES, MOD^R.

From the Proctor's man, to my horror, I learned,
that I was to *open* the schools—in other words,
that I was to keep the first *Act* of the year—a distinction for which I was indebted, not to any
merits of my own, but to the accident of being
of the same college with the *Senior* Proctor[1]. I
hastened in great alarm to my friend Hartley, and
consulted him on the best mode of proceeding.
I was taken completely by surprise, and was
anxious to put off the evil day as long as possible,
on account of being so wholly unprepared to meet
it. He dissuaded me from the attempt, and advised
me to confine my reading entirely to the subject
which I intended to keep, and that, having nothing
to do himself, he should have it in his power to
give me some material assistance. I applied to the

---

[1] Candidates for the B.A. degree were required by
statute to perform certain exercises in the schools which
were known as Acts and Opponencies. These exercises are
fully described in the *University Calendar* for 1802, pp. xiv–
xvii.

Dean for a "dormiat[1]", on account of having a bad cold, as I purposed reading very late at night. This indulgence was very readily granted me, and I enjoyed this privilege for a considerable time, except on Sunday mornings, when prayers began at a later hour.

It was very clear that Parkinson had not given the Moderators a very flattering account of my progress in my studies, as the Opponents assigned me were men scarcely known in the University, although two of them were afterwards Fellows of colleges. I waited upon the Moderator with my questions, which were the second and third sections of Newton, and Paley on Utility. I read intensely hard till the time of keeping my Act arrived, and with the aid of my kind friend (without whom I should have done nothing), I became tolerably master of my subjects. Jones was evidently surprised to find that I knew more of my questions than he had been led to expect. Towards the latter end of my thesis, I began to be alarmed, and my voice failed me; but before we had finished our discussion on the first argument, I recovered my self-possession, and retained it during the whole disputation. I understood the arguments of my Opponents much better than they did themselves, and disposed of them without much difficulty.

---

[1] Permission to be absent from morning chapel.

When the disputation ended, Jones dismissed me with the following compliment, which was *then* considered very honourable: "Tu, domine respondens, satis et optime quidem, et in Thesi, et in Disputatione, tuo officio functus es". An instance now and then occurred (I believe it happened at one of Brinkley's Acts), that a Respondent was complimented with the words "Summo ingenii acumine disputasti"; but in general ,"Optime quidem" was the highest honour bestowed. A year or two after this, Lax introduced the custom of giving to the disputants very high-flown compliments, and at the same time extending the disputations to double the usual length, which was about an hour and ten minutes. Both practices were disapproved of by those who took an interest in the disputations, and particularly by the Moderators of former years.

It is a very remarkable fact, that during the short time the disputations lasted, the Moderators were enabled to form a correct opinion of the disputants; but I can state, from actual observation, that for many years no man was ever a Wrangler who was not placed in the first or second class; and it generally (though not invariably) happened that a first-class man was placed higher on the Tripos than a man in the second class. Once, indeed, I knew a first-class man who was only fourth senior Optime; and I am not willing to allow that he was not so high as he ought to have been*, as *I* was the Examiner who had to settle the bracket of the first six senior Optimes.

The morning after my Act, Parkinson sent for me, and congratulated me most cordially, and I am sure most sincerely, on my success, which he acknowledged he had not expected. During that term my time was a good deal taken up in preparing for my Opponencies, of which I had three. A custom then prevailed, that the Respondent should invite his Opponents to drink tea with him, and they, in their turns, did the same. At the last meeting the Respondent left the room very early, and the Opponents compared their arguments, so that if possible the same objection should not be twice brought forward. Till within three or four years of that time these tea-drinkings had been wine-drinkings; but a member of the University, afterwards highly distinguished†, though at that time better known for his mathematical and philo-

---

* I was asked, when entering the Senate House the morning the brackets came out, to settle a bracket, which included six persons, who were at the head of the senior Optimes. Middleton, of Pembroke (afterwards Bishop of Calcutta), was among them. I was very reluctantly obliged to place him *fourth*: this he never forgave, but complained as long as he remained at college of my unfairness in asking questions above his comprehension. I much regretted his adherence to this opinion, for I had always been on good terms with him, and looked upon him as one of the most agreeable men of his time.

† Dr James Wood, Master of St John's.

sophical knowledge than for his social and convivial
qualities, suffered so severely from excess at one of
these meetings that the *wine-drinking* was discontinued. On one of these occasions an Opponènt, of
the name of Hargreaves, of St John's, received us
at the rooms of a friend; he apologised for not entertaining us at his own rooms, which could not, he
said, contain so large a party. He kept in what was
then called *The Tub*, to which you were admitted
by a trap-door in the floor.

The following term, Hartley being summoned
into Yorkshire by the illness of a relation, I should
have relapsed into my usual idle habits, had not
Parkinson urged me to prepare for my second Act.
By his desire I went to him one hour every other
day, and we read Newton together, particularly
the ninth and the eleventh sections. The latter
subject was entirely new to me, and I acknowledge,
with gratitude, that by his illustrations he rendered it highly interesting. When the Commencement arrived, I went home as usual, and for a short
time applied myself very closely; but towards the
end of August my studies were interrupted by an
intermittent fever (then only known by the name
of ague), which attacked all my brothers and
sisters. They were all cured, except my eldest
sister, by the use of Peruvian bark, which was then
considered a specific for that disease; but my poor
sister's disorder soon assumed a different character,

and she died about the middle of September. She was one year younger than myself, and I was much attached to her. This melancholy event affected my spirits greatly, and I looked forward with gloomy apprehension to the ensuing January. Could I have been sure of being placed (without keeping any more exercises in the schools) in the first or second class, I believe I should have practised what was afterwards done by men who were classed higher than they deserved, and who availed themselves of a *convenient* indisposition to take what was called an Ægrotat Senior Optime*.

I returned to college early in October, and prepared for my second Act. My questions were the ninth and eleventh sections of Newton, and the Credibility of Miracles. The Moderator was Professor Wollaston, who was extremely well satisfied, and dismissed me with—*Satis et optime omnes Quæstiones defendisti*. I did not leave college until after my degree, and read intensely during the whole time. Although I usually went to bed very late, I never suffered myself to sleep until I had passed in review the whole of what I had read in the day and evening. At first I found it very irksome, but I also found it very advantageous; what

Vol. I, *pp.* 79– 87

* Men who were placed in the first or second class by the Moderators were allowed this degree without further examination: this privilege was very frequently abused, and is now very properly abolished.

I thus reviewed was indelibly impressed on my mind, and I strongly recommend the practice. Three or four days before the examination, when I had entrenched myself in my own room for the night, Brinkley with two other friends shouted loudly for admission. He came to announce the unexpected tidings that I was in the first class, and to summon me to his rooms to play a rubber. I accompanied them to Caius, after having informed Hartley of this important event. Hartley was with me the next morning before I had risen, bringing under his arm the "Meditationes Algebraicæ" of Waring, six of whose forms he said it was absolutely necessary I should make myself acquainted with, as some of them would be sure to be set amongst the Evening Problems. A few days before the January term, the classes were always published by agreement between the Moderators, and few instances ever occurred in which persons placed by them below the first or second class ever became Wranglers; indeed, as only the first and second classes were allowed to go to the Moderators' rooms on the Monday and Tuesday evenings, when the examination by problems was considered the most difficult, it was almost impossible that those in the third or inferior classes could gain a higher degree than that of senior Optime. I recollect that in this year Wilby of St John's was in the third class, but was allowed the privilege of coming to the Moderators, because it was considered his position was owing to extreme deafness. As soon as he had entered, John Owen, of Bene't, who was also in the third class, attempted to follow, but was stopped by Wollaston, who explained to him the reason for admitting Wilby. After great altercation, Owen was allowed to pass. This circumstance caused much discussion, and in the result the papers of both were rejected. Wilby was eighteenth Wrangler, and Owen third senior Optime[1].

Monday, the first day of examination, at length arrived, and as soon as St Mary's clock struck nine I hastened to Trinity College, where (in B No. 2) I found breakfast prepared by my excellent friends Whaley Armitage and his cousin Robert Thornton; with them I breakfasted during the whole of the examination, and their anxiety for my success almost surpassed my own. I was so completely occupied on the Monday and Tuesday, that the days seemed neither long nor unpleasant; and even during the evenings, at the Moderators' rooms, we had no cause for complaint, for although we found the problems were more difficult than those we had during the day, we were most hospitably regaled by the Moderators (Wood and Wollaston), who had ordered an admirable dessert to be placed on

January 1788

---

[1] A description of the Senate House Examination is to be found in the *University Calendar* for 1802, pp. xvii–xliv.

the sideboard, and some very excellent wine. At Wollaston's rooms, the first and second problems were for the extraction of the square and cube roots, and what was never before heard of, every one *was required to attempt them as far as three places of Decimals.*

Wednesday, having no employment, except an hour's examination in Locke and Paley, I found extremely tedious. In self-defence I was obliged to have recourse to *Teetotum,* which was carried on with great spirit below stairs by considerable numbers, *during the whole of the examination.* On Thursday the brackets appeared. In the first were "Brinkley and Outram"; in the second, "Gunning, Vickers, Winthrop". Parkinson called me aside, and wished me very much to subject our bracket to a still further examination, telling me, *in confidence,* that I was the *last* in that bracket, and therefore could not lose, though I might be a gainer by the challenge. I assured him that my situation was so much higher than I had ever ventured to hope for —and could only be attributed to a fortunate concurrence of circumstances—that it would be highly imprudent in me to venture upon an additional examination. When I went into the Senate House, I should have felt perfectly happy if I could have been certain of being included in the list of Wranglers; in the course of it, however, my expectations were considerably raised, and I should

have been much disappointed if I had found myself at the bottom of the list. As soon as the
brackets were announced, Winthrop, whose serenity
and cheerfulness during the whole of the examination were the envy of us all, fell into a fit, and was
carried out of the Senate House in a state to alarm
all his friends. The expression of his medical attendant was, "He is in a perfect *deliquium* both of
body and mind". He recovered perfectly during
the day, and was admitted to his degree the
following morning in the usual manner.

Milner had been called upon to examine Brinkley
and Outram; the examination lasted some time,
for although no one doubted that Brinkley would
be Senior Wrangler, yet Outram's attainments
were of a very high order. In giving his decision,
Milner paid many high and well-merited compliments to the unsuccessful candidate. The examination was conducted with great seriousness and
decorum on this occasion; but it not unfrequently
happened that, when examining the brackets,
Milner was in the habit of indulging in jokes at the
expense of those unfortunate men who, when dissatisfied with their situation, had caused him to be
called in. Milner had a very loud voice, combined
with a peculiar shrillness, by which he could make
himself heard at a considerable distance. He was
in the habit of calling dull and stupid men *sooty
fellows*; and when he had a class of that description

to examine, he would call out to the Moderators, who were at the other end of the Senate House, "In rebus *fuliginosis* versatus sum".

Among the Moderators and Examiners of that day, Milner had and continued to have, during many years, a prodigious influence, and was frequently called upon to settle the places of men in the higher brackets. Being a man of strong nerves, and caring very little about the opinions of others, he got into frequent disputes with the Prælectors of colleges who ventured to remonstrate with him on the positions in which their men were placed on the Tripos. I well remember one occasion, upon which the Tutor of a college having in vain endeavoured to prevail upon him to place one of his pupils in a higher situation, at length said to him with much warmth, "Do you mean to say, Sir, that the man you have placed above my pupil *deserves* to be above him?"

Milner replied with much coolness, "I said no such thing; I only said that he *should stand above him!*"

For some years after he had ceased to be Moderator or Examiner, he was applied to on the Thursday when the brackets came out, to decide the positions of those men as to whose merits the Examiners had not made up their minds: on these occasions, except when a man of his own college or of Magdalene was concerned, I do not recollect to

have heard any well-founded charge of partiality
brought against him. He had ceased to be private
tutor, and was, therefore, very little interested in
the success of any particular person; his talents
and his power of discrimination were never called
in question; in short, as a learned prelate in his
Commencement speech as Regius Professor of
Divinity, when speaking of Milner as the editor of
his deceased brother's Church History, remarked,
he possessed every requisite for the office he had
undertaken, "præter æquitatem".

On the 18th of January, we were admitted *ad
respondendum quæstioni*. The admission of the
Bachelors took place without the least interruption. Our University at that time prided itself that
in this respect our practice was diametrically opposite to that of our sister University, at which on
all public occasions the entrance of the University
officers, and of persons distinguished by their rank
and station, was greeted either by shouts of applause, or by hissings and hootings. Sorry am I to
observe that for many years past the conduct of
our undergraduates has become more outrageous
than that of the Oxonians. It has not unfrequently happened that the Proctors have been
obliged to clear the galleries entirely, and it *has*
happened that the Vice-Chancellor has been under
the necessity of adjourning the proceedings; for

not only have the University authorities, whose
conduct has been thought to be marked by harsh-
ness and severity, been hissed and hooted, but
even private individuals whose supposed opinions
(whether political or religious) were disagreeable
to the majority, have been received with marked
insult. On this account the election of Vice-Chancellor, which used to take place in the afternoon, is
now constantly completed at an early hour in the
morning. After admission to their degrees, the
Bachelors generally assembled in large parties to
dinner, when everybody was obliged to swallow
a considerable quantity of bad wine. The same
evening at our college, and I believe in many
others in the University, the Bachelors invited the
Fellows to meet them at supper in the combination
room, which invitation all the Fellows made a
point of accepting. A handsome supper was provided, immense bowls of punch were emptied, and
every one was compelled to sing a song or to drink
an enormous glass of liquor by way of penalty.
These disgraceful proceedings were carried on to
a very late hour; and it was generally understood
that no man should be called to account for anything he said or did on so joyful an occasion. On
the following evening the Father of the college gave
a similar treat to the same parties, which was
conducted much in the same manner. I am
happy to say that these disgraceful meetings have

in our college, for some years past, fallen into
disuse.

[In January, 1788, Gunning left Cambridge for
Kingsland in Herefordshire, where he acted as a
tutor to the two sons of a Mr Evans. He returned
to Cambridge with his two pupils in the following
November.]

The next day, just as we were going to dinner *Vol. I*
(half-past one), I received a message from Mr *pp.* 103–
Thackeray, requesting me to go immediately to 107
his house. I was there informed that my poor Nov.
father was no more; he had walked once round the 1788
garden with my mother after breakfast, and on re-
entering the house, he soon after expired without
a groan. I hastened to Triplow, and after making
arrangements with my mother respecting the
funeral, came back to Cambridge the same evening
to give the necessary directions. Commending my
pupils to the especial care of my friend Hartley, I
returned to the vicarage, where I remained till after
the funeral. The living was immediately given to
Mr Berry, a Conduct Fellow of Trinity College,
and Curate of Great St Mary's. He desired my
mother to put herself to no inconvenience in leaving
the house, as it was not his intention to come into
residence till Lady-day. On returning to college,
in addition to the two Evans, I got, through the
kindness of Parkinson, several other pupils. When

the term ended, I went back to Triplow, and passed my Christmas holidays and the entire month of January with my mother and family. My father had died without a will, and my mother was left with eight children, of whom I (then in my twenty-first year) was the eldest. In the spring of the year, my mother and her family removed to Grantchester. About Easter, Parkinson sent for me, and said he had had a long conversation with Mr Wall, our Senior Fellow, of which I had been the subject. Mr Wall told him that he never intended to quit college, so that my chance of a fellowship was very remote. Parkinson added, that it had been settled between them that he should write a letter to the Bishop of Ely, strongly recommending me to his Lordship as a fit person to fill the fellowship of St John's, in his Lordship's gift, which was likely soon to be vacant by the promotion of Mr Hitch, who then held it; he said that no time should be lost, and advised me to put into the Bishop's hand, the following morning, a letter which he would immediately write on my behalf. I went to Ely early the next morning, and presenting myself at the palace, was courteously received by Dr Yorke, who was then Bishop; he said many civil things to me, but concluded by expressing his regret, that he could not appoint me to the fellowship, as he had resolved on giving it to his son, whom he designed for the Church. I was

about to take my leave, when, as if the thought
had suddenly struck him, he added, "I think I
shall be able to serve you; I can get your mother
and her family one of the houses appropriated to
the widows of clergymen in my diocese". Those who
remember that these houses were situated in the
most disreputable part of Cambridge, and that
no person of either sex could be seen there after
dark without exciting suspicion, and as three of
my mother's family were daughters, may easily
imagine that I declined his Lordship's *liberal* offer
with anything but expressions of gratitude; I did
not even attempt to conceal my surprise and indignation at his proposal. I returned to Cambridge,
and recounted to Parkinson all that had passed.
He regretted my disappointment, and comforted
me by the assurance that I should not want for
pupils if he could procure them for me. Dr Fisher,
who was an advocate in the Commons, and one of
our Senior Fellows, offered me without solicitation
the use of his rooms, which were in the New
Building, and completely though plainly furnished;
he would not hear of any remuneration, and im-
posed only one condition, that if he or any of his
friends should wish to reside there, I should give
them up at a short notice. I lived in them four years,
during which time he came into residence but once,
and then only for about a week.

After the Commencement, I returned to my

family at Grantchester, where I divided my time between fishing and reading. The river from Coe Fen to Hauxton Mills abounded with fish, and the Rev. Mr Pemberton, who lived in the Manor-house, gave every encouragement to anglers (whom he spoke of as the true descendants of Izaak Walton); but he did all in his power to put a stop to the use of nets. The descendants of Izaak were not very numerous; I do not think there were ten men in the University who were regular anglers. Ben Sheppard, of King's and Alexander Cotton, afterwards Rector of Girton, were the most constant.

At the Summer Assizes of this year, two members of the University surrendered themselves to take their trials for the murder of a drayman, in a row between "Town and Gown", in the preceding March. The indictment against them was thrown out by the Grand Jury, and the Coroner's inquisition quashed for informality. The person who actually struck the blow (of which the drayman was said to have died) was Thomas Taylor, of Trinity, whom I was frequently in the habit of meeting: he went by the name of "Turk Taylor", as he used to boast that he was to occupy a very high situation at Constantinople as soon as he had taken his degree. Although he was a man of dissolute and extravagant habits, he was far from being unkind or vindictive in his disposition; and when this unfortunate circumstance occurred, he was as

much pitied as blamed. He was deeply in debt
when he left the University, and was not heard of
for many years. Tom Hart, who had been Vice-
Provost of King's, and afterwards took the living
of Ringwood, in Hampshire, told me that when he
was at dinner one day, he was called out by the
urgent entreaties of a poor man lying in a pass-
cart, apparently in a dying state: this man was
Taylor, whom he had known as the gayest of the
gay, and constantly associating with noblemen and
men of rank in the University.

Section ii

ESQUIRE BEDELL

Vol. I,
pp. 123–
125
Sept.
1789

As I was too young to take orders, it was suggested by some of my friends that I should be a candidate for the Bedellship[1]; and as I knew the Vice-Chancellor, Dr Barnes, always rose between five and six, I determined to be the first to apply to him. He had been an intimate friend of my father, to whom for many years he had paid an annual visit at Christmas, and had known me from my childhood. He promised me his support without hesitation, and said that as soon as he had breakfasted he would call upon his brother Heads, and solicit them in my favour. Having secured the Vice-Chancellor, I called on Parkinson, who promised to do everything in his power for me, and canvass such of the Fellows as were in residence. Thus supported, I waited upon the Master of Christ's (Dr Barker), and as he was not at home, I informed Mrs Barker of my intention. She heartily wished me success, and offered to call on several persons in the University with whom I was but slightly acquainted—and she lost no time in performing her promise. In two or three instances, when I subsequently called upon these persons

[1] Francis Dawes, Fellow of Peterhouse and one of the Esquire Bedells, committed suicide in September 1789.

(whom I was in no hurry to visit, as I thought myself secure of them), they observed that I was too late, as they had already promised their votes: they did not, however, suffer me to leave their rooms till they informed me it was Mrs Barker who had forestalled my application. After canvassing the whole morning, I never failed to go to the theatre, as I felt quite sure that if any elector had arrived that evening, I should meet with him there. When I returned home one evening, I found a note from Mr Mortlock, dated Christ's Lodge: he told me he was dining there, that he should not be able to quit very early, but would give me a call as soon as he could get away. He came about twelve o'clock, informed me he had heard at the Lodge I was a candidate for the Bedellship, and that he thought he could do me some service. He wrote in my room that night several notes to resident members of the University with whom he was on intimate terms. He told me he was going to Wood-bridge very early the following morning, and as he travelled on horseback, he could call on several electors, without deviating much from his direct route, and that he thought he could procure their votes for me. He gave me a list of their names. He performed his promise to the very letter, and sent me a detailed account of the result of his applications, which was much in my favour.

Vol. I,
*pp.*129–
139

The other candidates for the Bedellship were Thomas Emly, a Fellow of King's, M.A. in 1783, and a Licentiate in Medicine; Mr Lamb, Fellow of St John's, who took his Bachelor's degree in 1786; and Mr Eamonson, Fellow of Catharine Hall, M.A. in 1775, who had unsuccessfully opposed Mr Mathew for the same office in that year. The election was fixed for the 13th of October, the nomination necessarily taking place the morning before. Mr Eamonson and myself were nominated. Railroads and electric telegraphs were at that time not even dreamed of, and elections when a nomination took place were determined (as the founders of our statutes probably intended) by the votes of the resident members, and those within a few miles of the University.

I had met with great encouragement in my canvass. The Johnians promised me their support, provided their own man was not nominated; the men of Trinity were (with few exceptions) against me, as Eamonson had taken his degree at that college. At Emmanuel I had the votes of all the Fellows; and the Master fixed the audit the day before the election, that the Fellows might not have the trouble of a second journey. The Provost and Fellows of King's were all with me; for their support I was indebted to Dr Barnes, the Vice-Chancellor. The members of my own college came up at the request of the Master and Tutors. I was elected by a majority of two to one, the numbers being 112 to 56. Many were the offers to pair off in my favour, and my opponent had a great number who offered to support him in the same manner. We came, however, to a mutual agreement not to allow pairs on either side. I was then a novice in election matters; but I thought that when a pair took place, there was not unfrequently some trickery on one side or the other, sometimes on both. Subsequent experience has fully confirmed the correctness of the opinion I then formed.

I went the morning after my election to the rooms of my excellent friend and colleague, William Mathew (Senior Fellow and Bursar of Jesus College), to ask him to instruct me in the duties of my office. "They lie in small compass", said he, "and are soon learned. The art of *carving* we are required to understand *well*, being so constantly called upon to practise it. No man breathing is better skilled in this department than Beverley. He knows the best cuts in a joint, but cannot bear to send them *all* away; he therefore manages to be disputing with one or another during dinner-time, and as nothing puts him out of countenance, he laughs at all remarks, and puts the best slices on his own plate. He stood a little in awe of Dawes, but now that he is no more, he will help about half-a-dozen at the head of the table, and then put the knife into your hands or mine."

Mathew then proceeded to state what he considered the most important part of our duty, viz. *punctuality*. "The statutes of the University", he said, "enjoin the Respondent to dispute from the *first* to the *third* hour. The authorities consider the statutes to be complied with, provided the disputant is in the box *before* the clock strikes two, and does not leave until after it strikes three. By the statutes", he added, "a person preaching *ad clerum*, must preach a *nonâ usque ad undecimam horam*. In point of practice, the statute is considered to be complied with if the Preacher be in the *vestry* before the clock has actually struck ten. In the same way, a Congregation fixed for eleven o'clock is considered to begin at ten, at which hour the Congregation bell begins. There are other points of practice", he added, "which are soon learned"—and, I very shortly discovered, were as soon forgotten. As most of these were founded *on a violation of the statutes*, I inserted them in a memorandum-book, and Mathew permitted me to copy from his book remarks he had previously made.

When I called upon Dr Pennington to thank him for the assistance he had given me, he asked if I had made myself acquainted with the duties of my office. I told him that my colleague, Mathew, had promised me assistance, and I hoped with that and my own observation to be soon acquainted with everything that was required. "Your duties", he said, "are three-fold: attendance on the Vice-Chancellor, attendance on the University, and '*Otium*'": this he explained by informing me, that one week in three I should have no duties at all. Agreeable as this information was to a man naturally indolent, I did not avail myself of it, and although residing in the country, I made a point of being present on all occasions, that I might not lay myself open to the charge of living away from the University. I was never absent unless unavoidably prevented from attending.

By the death of Dawes, Beverley had become Senior Bedell. He took his Bachelor's degree at Christ's College in 1767; his name is not to be found on either Tripos[1]; and if his own account of himself is to be believed (and perhaps *in this instance* his word may be taken), he was one of the most profligate men in the University. He was the son of a wine-merchant at Norwich, and used to relate, with great glee, the mode in which he disposed of a pipe of port for his father, by persuading him that he was so popular amongst the undergraduates, that he could dispose of a pipe amongst his own friends without the least difficulty. Whether he succeeded in selling the wine, I know not; but he never failed

---

[1] There were two Tripos papers: on the first appeared the names of the Wranglers and senior Optimes, on the second the names of the junior Optimes.

to add, that he took effectual care that none of the
money should ever reach his father.

When Beverley first became a candidate for the
Bedellship, he was opposed by Mr Richard Hey of
Magdalene College, a man of high character and
reputation; he had been third Wrangler and senior
medallist in 1768. Beverley succeeded through the
influence of Lord Sandwich, who had made himself
very popular in the county and in the University,
by giving a series of splendid entertainments at
Christmas whilst at Hinchinbrooke Castle.

Beverley married early, and had a numerous
family; he lived in a most extravagant manner, and
was always in pecuniary difficulties. To extricate
himself from them he had a variety of expedients;
he would dispose of musical instruments and choice
flowers (of which he really had a fine collection) at
a very high price, by means of a *lottery*, to obtain
subscriptions for which he and his friends can-
vassed the members of the University. Beverley
would often boast of his great intimacy with the
"Heads of Houses", of which he used to give the
following proof, that, with the exception of two or
three, he had borrowed money of them all, in sums
varying from ten guineas to a hundred; and as they
well knew he could never repay them, the lending
him money was a proof of their personal regard for
him. Upon one occasion, he evaded the just de-
mands of a poor butcher by pleading the statute of

limitations. The public were so fully satisfied of the justice of the demand, that a subscription was raised for the claimant; and Dr Glyn, who told me the story, added, "I have never spoken to the scoundrel since".

When I became a candidate for my present office, he voluntarily offered to support me by his vote and interest, professing a very great respect for my father and grandfather. A few days after my election, he informed me that there were certain sums of money (for hearing the Masters of Arts read Greek, &c.) which were to be divided equally between the Bedells, but which it was the privilege of the Senior Bedell to collect. He said, with apparent frankness, "I tell you honestly, that I am not to be trusted with money; now I will propose that our colleague, Mathew, who is one of the most honourable and amiable of men, should receive these fees". To this I most readily assented, as there was but one opinion respecting the merits of Mathew. Four or five years elapsed without a word being said respecting these receipts. I mentioned to Mathew my intention of marrying, when he said to me, "Has Beverley paid you any money on account of the fees he has received?" I answered in the negative, and related the conversation which had taken place between Beverley and myself on the subject. He replied, "'Tis exactly as I apprehended, and I take shame to myself for not having mentioned it to you sooner. For my own part, being an old bachelor, and a Fellow of a college, the loss is of little consequence; but I ought to have put you on your guard, and have told you that Beverley never refunds". In consequence of this conversation, I called upon Beverley for an account of the sums received by him. He repeatedly promised to send it me; he never did so. Mathew and I made out the best account we could from the Registrary's books: he owed me between seventy and eighty pounds. Those who knew Beverley will not be surprised to hear that I never received one shilling of this sum.

The death of Mathew, which took place a few years after I came into office, was a very unfortunate circumstance for the University, and to me the loss was irreparable. The few Heads who had usually been considered the expounders of our statutes, and who, whenever a difficulty arose, were applied to for a solution, were either dead or too infirm to attend Congregations. Beverley, as Senior Bedell, was always at hand to answer questions; and whenever I ventured to remonstrate with him on the incorrectness of our proceedings, would answer me in the most abrupt manner, saying, "How is it possible you should know anything about it, when you are only just elected?" Equally disgusted with his ignorance and his arrogance, I suffered the proceedings to go on without further interruption; and it not unfrequently happened, at the close of a Congregation, for Borlase (the Registrary) to remark to me, "I presume you are aware, everything that has been done this morning is unstatutable". To this remark it was impossible not to assent. Beverley's popularity amongst the Heads was increased by his conduct respecting Frend's trial, where he acted as, and received the emoluments of, a Proctor of the Court; and he persuaded many that had it not been for his strenuous exertions, and superior knowledge regarding the forms of proceeding, the ends of justice would have been defeated, and Frend obtained a triumph. But what, perhaps, rendered Beverley more especially popular, was the reputation he possessed of being a great favourite with the First Lord of the Admiralty, who had appointed him Commissioner and Comptroller of an office in Greenwich Hospital.

During the Christmas holidays, his Lordship was in the habit of giving a series of splendid entertainments at Hinchinbrooke Castle, where Beverley was supposed to be master of the revels. He possessed considerable musical talents, and played on the double-bass, an instrument on which, at that time, there were but few professors. At the concerts given on these occasions, the musical talents of Joah Bates, then a Scholar at King's, and afterwards the celebrated conductor of the concerts in

Westminster Abbey in commemoration of Handel, first became known.

Beverley wished it to be understood that he was always consulted by Lord Sandwich, as to what members of the University should be invited to those parties, at which the Prince of Wales and many of the most distinguished men of the day were to be present; and he, at the same time, hinted very broadly that there *was a way* to obtain his recommendation. In a subsequent dispute between him and Harwood about money matters, Beverley asserted that twenty guineas, which he acknowledged to have received from Harwood, was not lent, but given as a gratuity for procuring him invitations to Hinchinbrooke. It was well known that Beverley was always in difficulties, and that he never missed the opportunity of getting money from any available source. He had taken repeated advantage of Dr Jowett's enthusiasm for music, by borrowing sums of money which he never repaid. The Doctor at last, when much pressed for the further loan of ten guineas, refused to lend it unless the double-bass was pledged as security. This was agreed to, and Beverley was allowed the use of it at musical entertainments, the Doctor's servants being in attendance to carry it back to Trinity Hall, at the termination of the concert.

Notwithstanding Beverley's character being so well known, it was quite clear that for many years he carried on the business of the University in the Senate House, in perfect contempt of the statutes and of its approved usages. The case I am about to mention was one of very common occurrence. After having received the Graces from the Vice-Chancellor, he gave them to me to take to the Lower House[1]; when they had been read, I carried them back to him, and he sometimes discovered that not one-half of them had been delivered to me, but were left in his coat pocket. This mistake was sometimes not discovered until the afternoon Congregation, but he proceeded with the business as if everything had been correctly done in the morning. Although my office in the Senate House was thus made merely ministerial, I failed not to note down the number of voters on any material question, and the causes which led to its concession or rejection. I also kept an account of the decisions of the Heads on any disputed point—a case which very rarely occurred, as, when a difficulty presented itself, Beverley stepped forward with his usual effrontery, and said he well remembered how it had been decided on a similar occasion.

On September the 5th, an election took place of an Esquire Bedell, in the room of William Mathew, *Vol. II, pp. 70– 72. 1797*

---

[1] The Senate was then divided into two houses of Regents and Non-Regents, the latter being styled the Lower House.

LL.B., Fellow and Bursar of Jesus College, deceased.

The death of this amiable and excellent man was to me a source of great discomfort; and for many years I had very weighty reasons for lamenting him. We had been on terms of the most intimate friendship, which a difference of opinion on political subjects never interrupted for a single moment. In all difficulties I applied to him for advice, and so sound did I consider his judgment that I invariably followed it. The respectability of his character prevented the office (which Mr Beverley was constantly degrading by his conduct) from sinking in the estimation of the University. To me it was an object of deep importance that his successor should be a man of such talents and acquirements as to entitle him to the respect and consideration of the University. Such a candidate appeared in the person of John Ellis, Esq., M.A., a Fellow of King's College: he had been a travelling Bachelor, and was thrown by Buonaparte into a French prison, from which one of his letters to the University is dated. He was a man of gentlemanly manners, and a general favourite with all his acquaintance. His opponent was Charles Isola, B.A. of Emmanuel College, the son of Agostino Isola, a teacher of Italian in this town. The father was generally beloved, particularly by his pupils, who were very numerous. There was a great desire amongst the members of the University, particularly amongst those of his own college, to do something for his son, who was a man of inoffensive manners, and had not, I believe, an enemy in the world; but his shyness and reserve were so great that it pained him to mix in society.

I was induced, both from my friendship to the man and my regard for the office, to support Ellis, though by doing so I gave great offence to many whom I highly valued.

At the election Isola was chosen by a large majority, the numbers being for Isola, 94; for Ellis, 42.

We held office together for sixteen years in the most perfect harmony. I found him kind and accommodating, and ready to undertake all the duties that did not include the necessity of dining in a large party, to which he had an insuperable objection.

It was with much regret I followed him to his grave; and sorry was I to discover, a few days afterwards, that George Ware, M.A., of St John's College, must inevitably be his successor, as there was no other candidate; and such was the disesteem into which the office had fallen from Beverley's conduct, that the Heads were under the necessity of requesting Mr (afterwards Dr) Haviland to allow his name to be returned to the Senate in conjunction with Mr Ware.

Vol. II,
pp. 311–
315.
1821

Having for some time experienced that the duties of my office were beyond my capability of performing satisfactorily, Beverley having for several years lived principally in London, and Ware being worse than inefficient, I complained to the Heads, who agreed to pay 100*l.* a-year to a deputy, provided Beverley *resided* altogether away from Cambridge. A Bachelor of Arts of St John's College, named William John Smith, was selected for that purpose by Beverley. The Grace for his appointment was opposed in the Regent-house, and was carried by a majority of only one, Beverley being in that majority. After his election, I frankly told him that though I had voted against him, yet, as the Senate had thought proper to elect him, I wished to be on good terms, and would do all in my power to make his situation comfortable. He was married before he took his degree, and his income was supposed to be derived from his situation as reporter to the "Cambridge Chronicle".

Dr Wordsworth was at this time Vice-Chancellor; and when I met Smith at Trinity Lodge, the Sunday following his election, he accosted me in these words: "Do you know what the Heads met for yesterday?" I replied, that "I never knew what the Heads met for until their proceedings became public". The instant the Vice-Chancellor entered the room, he said to him, "I understand there was a meeting of the Heads yesterday"; and, before the astonished Vice-Chancellor could give an answer, he proceeded—"any particular business that called them together?"

"The Heads are never called together except on particular business", was the reply of the Vice-Chancellor, delivered in his most solemn tone. I took an opportunity, soon after we returned from church, of telling Smith that if he went on as he had commenced, he would not long remain in office; and I added, that I had held my situation upwards of thirty years, and that though I had been on intimate terms with several of the Vice-Chancellors, I had never ventured to ask such a question.

Returning from church in the afternoon, and finding we could not make satisfactory progress on account of the number of Masters of Arts who crowded the pavement by St Michael's, he shouted out, at the top of his voice, "Make way for the Vice-Chancellor!"

From the above instances it may be inferred he was not p   ticularly well qualified for the office; in fact, I was heartily ashamed of my new colleague. With the vulgarity of Ware, he combined a flippant assurance peculiarly his own. He, however, contrived to hold th   appointment for three years.

After a visit of the Chancellor to the University, Smith detailed to me, with considerable and as I thought unnecessary minuteness, the festivities at which we had both been present. I set him right in several particulars relative to the station and rank of many of the guests. Taking out his tablets, he requested me to repeat my observations, for he wished to be accurate, as he was reporting for the London papers. I declined to be his assistant, and walked away. In a subsequent conversation, he informed me that, as one of *the gentlemen of the press*, he had introduced himself at the High Steward's at Wimpole, and also at Lord Braybrooke's; that at both these houses he had been allowed to take notes of everything worth recording: and he added, with great glee, that he had "fared most sumptuously in the steward's room!"

For some time Smith encouraged the belief, that he should be appointed to the office he was holding as deputy, when Beverley died. I assured him he had not the most remote chance, and I strongly urged him to resign at the expiration of the third year, or the probability was he would be superseded. He took my advice, and sent in his resignation, making, at the same time, a claim on the Vice-Chancellor for 200*l.*, which he asserted, with great pertinacity, he was out of pocket by being Beverley's deputy. His claim was laughed at, and he quitted the University.

The Honourable George Neville Grenville, Master of Magdalene, had employed Smith to decipher "Pepys's Diary"—not a very difficult task, as

Lord Grenville had furnished the alphabet. He was liberally rewarded for his trouble, but, according to his own estimate of his merits, not sufficiently so; for some time after, when he had obtained orders, a "puff direct" (no doubt through his previous connexion with the press) appeared in many of the papers. It began by complimenting Lord Braybrooke as the editor, and then proceeded in the following words: "But to whom are we indebted for deciphering this manuscript? We understand that the credit of it is entirely due to the Rev. W. J. Smith, *Curate* of ——, in Norfolk. And is this man still a Curate? It will be a disgrace to the Bench of Bishops if he long remain so." The Bishops, however, were as insensible to this as to all his other merits.

He subsequently managed to get introduced to Miss Martineau, in consequence of whose application, he was presented by Lord Brougham to a living in Norfolk.

Having most acutely felt the degradation of being obliged to associate with men whom I blush to recollect as my colleagues, I have a proud satisfaction in being able to record the entire restoration of the respectability of the office of Esquire Bedell, by the appointment in this year of George Leapingwell, M.A. of Corpus (the son of my old college friend, with whom, in my undergraduateship, I

Vol. II, pp. 334–335. 1826

had passed so many merry hours), and of William Hopkins, of Peterhouse, who was elected the following year. To these kind friends I am indebted for their considerate and generous conduct, in discharging between them my share of the duties of the office, from the time I became so entirely incapacitated by my accident.

Section iii

CHARACTERS

Dr Richard Farmer
Master of Emmanuel College

Dr Farmer was elected Master of Emmanuel on the death of Dr Richardson, in 1775, and shortly afterwards became Vice-Chancellor.

Vol. I, p. 159

He had a deep-rooted dislike of Dissenters, whom he was most anxious to exclude from office, because he *conscientiously* believed them to be disaffected to the existing Government; but to those men whom he believed to be sincere and disinterested in their opinions (however contrary to his own), he always behaved with fairness and impartiality. To me he was ever particularly kind, and never failed inviting me to the college feasts, which were numerous, and most strictly observed. He would sometimes make allusion, in a jocular manner, to my well-known political opinions; thus in taking up his pipe, he would balance it on his finger, and when it turned over he would say, "This is a Whig pipe, Master Gunning; it has got a twist the wrong way". For many years before he was elected to the Mastership he had the Curacy of Swavesey (about nine miles distant), where he made a point of attending in all weathers. He began the service

*Vol. I, pp.*162–170

punctually at the appointed time, and gave a plain practical sermon, strongly enforcing some moral duty. After service he chatted most affably with his congregation, and never failed to send some small present to such of his poor parishioners as had been kept from church through illness. After morning service he repaired to the public-house, where a mutton-chop and potatoes were soon set before him: these were quickly despatched, and immediately after the removal of the cloth, Mr Dobson (his churchwarden) and one or two of the principal farmers, made their appearance, to whom he invariably said, "I am going to read prayers, but shall be back by the time you have made the punch". Occasionally another farmer accompanied him from church, when pipes and tobacco were in requisition until six o'clock. *Taffy* was then led to the door, and he conveyed his master to his rooms by half-past seven; here he found his slippers and night-cap, and taking possession of his elbow-chair, he slept till his bed-maker aroused him at nine o'clock, when resuming his wig he started for the *Parlour*, where the Fellows were in the habit of assembling on a Sunday evening.

Having mentioned Sal Elvedge[1] as a specimen of college bed-makers, I feel inclined to introduce Dr Farmer's barber to my readers, as a fair sample

[1] See Gunning's *Reminiscences* (2nd Edition), vol. i, pp. 56–57: not included in these selections.

of college barbers, an important class of men at
that period. If the following anecdote should
offend "ears polite", its truthfulness must be my
excuse for recording it in my reminiscences of
college life "Sixty years since".

Bob Foster was a privileged man at Emmanuel;
he was a great retailer of news to Farmer, who
would occasionally amuse us with what he had
heard. One morning, when the barber was performing his accustomed office, he said in reply to
Farmer's remark—"Well! what news?" "I saw
Tom —— yesterday, and he made such a bad remark about you!" "What was it?" asked the
Doctor. "Indeed, Sir, I could not tell you; for it
was too bad to repeat!" Farmer still urged the
point, when the barber (having first obtained a
promise that his master would not be angry) replied with *much apparent reluctance*—"Why, Sir,
he said you wasn't fit to carry guts to a bear!"
"And what did you say?" asked Farmer. The barber replied with much energy and seeming satisfaction—"I said, Sir, that you was!"

It is probable, from what I have been relating
of Farmer, that an unfavourable opinion may be
formed of him as a country curate; but the truth
is, that most of the churches within ten miles of
Cambridge were served by Fellows of colleges. In
some cases the curate hastened back to dine in hall;
there were others who undertook two or three

services; so that, upon the whole, few parishes were
so well satisfied with their pastor as Swavesey.

During this period suppers were served in the
halls of several of the colleges. At Trinity they
were not abolished until after the death of Re-
nouard, the Vice-Master, who was a regular attendant, as also Carr the Bursar, and Pugh, the
Incumbent of Bottisham. In those colleges where
there were no suppers, the officiating clergy
formed Sunday-evening Clubs. At St John's it was
called "The Curates' Club". At King's, "The
Neck or Nothing", so named from the supper consisting of necks of mutton cut into chops. At
Christ's, the meeting was called "The Apostolic";
the supper was always tripe, dressed in various
ways. As many of the curates had dined early, and
fared but scantily, they enjoyed their suppers pro-
digiously. Each club was restricted to its own
members, but when Farmer became Master of his
college, Emmanuel Parlour, where he always presided on a Sunday evening, became greatly celebrated; for as Sunday was the usual day for visiting
the University, persons of any station, or literary
acquirement, would have considered their visit in-
complete unless they shared in the hospitalities of
Emmanuel Parlour, after having dined with the
Vice-Chancellor.

There was a frankness and heartiness about
Farmer that was particularly taking: he was just

as much at his ease with Cabinet Ministers as he
was with his own Fellows. Whenever Mr Pitt came
to visit his constituents, he was always particularly
affable; but unless Farmer was of the party, the
conversation soon became constrained and em-
barrassed. It was evident the rulers of the University could not forget they were in the presence of
a man who had the power of dispensing Bishoprics
and Deaneries; and it was this feeling probably
that caused them at times to be reserved and
obsequious, and at others, they seemed to endeavour to astonish the Premier by an elaborate,
but perhaps, at times, an unseasonable display of
erudition. As soon as Farmer joined them, the
scene assumed a different aspect, and a tone of
cheerfulness and hilarity succeeded the dulness
and solemnity which had previously marked the
meeting.

Porson used to remark, that all *original* wit was
but *quotation*, of which seeming paradox Farmer's
conversation furnished a very happy illustration.
He had Shakespeare and all the early dramatic
writers by heart, and whatever subject was introduced, he was enabled, from his richly stored mind,
immediately to produce something applicable. I
am not aware that he ever published anything but
a small pamphlet on the "Learning of Shakespeare", which completely settled that disputed
point.

That Pitt not only enjoyed his conversation, but had a great personal regard for Farmer, is indisputable; for the Premier could not give a stronger proof of his entire confidence in Farmer's judgment and integrity, than by asking his opinion and advice regarding the filling up the Mastership of Trinity, when vacant by the death of Dr Hinchliffe, Bishop of Peterborough. "If you wish to oblige the Society, appoint Postlethwaite," was the honest, the disinterested reply of Farmer. Pitt made the appointment on this recommendation, without any solicitation on the part of Postlethwaite.

It was about this period that a circumstance occurred which caused Farmer considerable uneasiness, nor did he ever completely get over it. It had been long whispered in the University, that Farmer had made proposals to a daughter of Sir Thomas Hatton; that he was accepted by the lady, but that the father (although on the most intimate terms with Farmer) positively refused his sanction to their marriage. When the Baronet died, it was fully expected that the engagement would be made public; but, to the surprise of all who knew the parties, it was terminated in a most unexpected manner. Farmer employed Harwood to communicate to the lady his change of sentiments. A more unsuitable ambassador could not have been selected to make a communication of so delicate a nature;

though it was a prevailing opinion that Farmer could scarcely have employed a more *willing* envoy, as Harwood was for the most part a resident at the Lodge, and his position there must have been considerably changed by Farmer's marriage. Both Harwood and Farmer were attacked with epigrams without end, to which (although the Public Orator could not miss so fair an opportunity of attacking Harwood) Tweddell was the principal contributor.

So sensible was Pitt of the value of Farmer's opinion, and so disinterested a counsellor had he always proved himself, that Pitt twice offered him a Bishopric, "which he did twice refuse". In declining this honour, he showed that he possessed that rarest of all knowledge—*self-knowledge*. He would have made, I have heard him remark, "a very indifferent Bishop". He felt he could not discharge the duties of the Episcopacy with that dignity and decorum which the office demanded: however, he eventually accepted a Residentiaryship of St Paul's, an appointment he considered far more suitable, and in which situation he was very popular. Consistently with his love of good fellowship, he gave excellent dinners to the Minor Canons on a Sunday, at one o'clock. In the evening a hot supper was always ready at nine, at which any friends from Cambridge, who chanced to be in town, were sure to meet with a hearty reception, and pass a convivial evening, which forcibly

served to remind them of the hospitalities of
Emmanuel Parlour. Farmer's mornings were
usually spent in examining the old book-stalls
in the neighbourhood of St Paul's. He seldom
travelled far west, and troubled himself but little
about politics. When I have said he was a decided
Tory, it is scarcely necessary to add he was a *High-
Churchman*; it being a modern discovery that the
principles held by the *Low-Church* party do not
clash with "the right divine of Kings to govern
wrong". His residence in town rarely prevented
his being present on Feast-days at his own college.
I well remember his exclaiming, on entering the
vestry at St Mary's on Ascension-Day,—"I have
had hard work to be with you in time, Mr Vice-
Chancellor, for at three o'clock this morning I was
blowing my pipe with the worshipful Company of
Pewterers!"

On the 29th of September, 1784, Emmanuel
College celebrated the 200th anniversary of its
foundation. The entertainment was of the most
superb description. Several lively turtles were to
be seen in tubs of water, at the Master's Lodge,
where the people were allowed for some days to
gratify their curiosity with a sight so novel at
Cambridge*. Upon this occasion (and which was

* Upon one occasion a woman who had been looking
at them very attentively, said, "Pray, Sir, are *them* real
turtles or mock turtles?"

ordinarily the custom in those days) there were many amateur singers amongst the members of the University. Dr Randall, Professor of Music, who shone as much in convivial as in musical talent, was called upon for his celebrated song in the character of a drunken man. The representation was so faithfully given, that Mr Pitt was completely deceived, and thinking him to be actually the "Great Sublime" he drew, expressed much anxiety lest the worthy Professor should meet with some accident when leaving the college. My father, who related this anecdote to me, also remarked that Pitt was the life and soul of the party; and although my father possessed the true Johnian feeling with regard to Townshend, he added that he was not at all surprised at Pitt having been returned the preceding April at the head of the poll; for his idea of the social talent of the Premier exactly accorded with the description given by Lord Euston, who was so frequently in the habit of meeting him in those small parties of his intimate friends, in whose society he seemed to forget the cares of office.

JEMMY GORDON

It was at the election in the summer of this year that Jemmy Gordon (afterwards a well-known character in the University) made his first appearance in the Senate House. His father was Chapel Clerk at Trinity, and a man of some pro-

Vol. I,
*pp.*173–
180.
1790

perty; he gave his son a good classical education, and afterwards articled him to a respectable attorney by the name of Haggerstone. At the expiration of his articles, he commenced practice in Freeschool Lane, in the house which ought to have been occupied by the Master of the Perse School, but which was at that time (through the neglect of the Trustees) let to the highest bidder: here he led an expensive and profligate life, and placed at the head of his table a young woman of considerable beauty, who went by the *sobriquet* of "the Duchess of Gordon".

Soon after the election commenced, Gordon entered the crowded Senate and joined Mr Pitt; he was handsomely dressed in the Windsor Livery, a blue coat with red cuffs and collar; he congratulated the Premier upon the triumph he was about to obtain, and censured in strong terms Mr Tharp, who had lately purchased the Chippenham estate, and was talked of as a candidate for the county—— "his presumption in coming forward!"—and could not understand "what claim his large possessions in Jamaica gave him to disturb the peace of the county of Cambridge!" He added that his influence (which he hinted was pretty considerable) should be exerted in support of the old members. He continued walking backwards and forwards, conversing with Mr Pitt, for about half-an-hour; those

who knew him were extremely indignant at his presumption, but no one liked to interfere. At length
Beverley undertook to have him turned out, and
walked up to him, attended by two constables, for
that purpose. Jemmy, finding it vain to resist,
made a hasty retreat. Mr Pitt was all astonishment to see his new friend, of whose loyalty and
good sense he had formed a very favourable
opinion, so unceremoniously treated. The crowd
below the barrier hustled him out of the Senate
House. Beverley, elated with his victory, followed,
and urged the persons assembled outside to take
him off and place him under the Conduit. Beverley's
zeal carried him beyond the steps of the Senate
House, where he soon found that Gordon had more
friends than himself. Gordon was immediately
rescued, and if the constables had not interfered,
Beverley would probably have undergone the
punishment he would so willingly have inflicted on
another.

Jemmy had at that time a cousin of the name of
Goode, who resided for a few terms at Trinity Hall;
he had been well educated, and was a remarkably
good-looking man, but his habits were low and
profligate. I do not recollect ever to have met him
in a party at Trinity Hall, or any other college; he
had, however, his friends in the University, and to
all those parties his cousin Jemmy was always a
welcome guest, for he sang a good song, told a good

story, had Horace at his fingers' ends, and was in the habit of quoting him with considerable effect.

Though Gordon realized but little by his profession, yet, as his father made him a handsome allowance, he used to give in his turn some very jovial entertainments at his own house; but his extravagance knew no bounds, and he was, after a time, under the necessity of going into cheap and obscure lodgings; for his means would not enable him to gratify his extraordinary fondness for wine and liquor. He was then at the service of any man who thought proper to send him an invitation to entertain his friends, and to get very drunk by way of recompense. Dressed in a huge cocked-hat, and the tarnished uniform of a general or an admiral (for Jemmy was *not too proud* to accept any article of apparel that was occasionally given to him from an old-clothes shop), he was to be heard about the streets, frequently until daylight, roaring out scraps of songs, or quoting fragments of poetry. A relation dying left him a guinea a-week, to be paid weekly, but it was soon deeply mortgaged. Spending every shilling he could get in liquor, he at length became so shabby and so dirty, that no one would suffer him to enter his rooms. As he was not ashamed to beg, he applied to every person he met, and raised money in that way; some giving because they believed him to be in distress; others because they were afraid of him; for if any person (no matter what his rank or position in Town or University might be) had been guilty of any indiscretion, Jemmy would be sure to proclaim it aloud whenever he met him. As he was known to have a very great objection to fighting, many men whom he insulted, preferred breaking his head to giving him half-a-crown, but these persons Jemmy contrived to render ultimately his most profitable customers; so that it might be said of him, as of the Grecian orator, ʿO γὰρ ἄνθρωπος οὐ κεφαλὴν, ἀλλὰ πρόσοδον κέκτηται*.

Passing through Trinity College one day, he saw the Bishop of Bristol walking backwards and forwards in front of his Lodge. Gordon accosted him in his usual strain, "I hope, my Lord, you will give me a shilling!" to this his Lordship replied, "If you can find me a greater scoundrel than yourself, I will give you half-a-crown". Jemmy made his bow, and shortly after meeting Beverley, said, "Have you seen a messenger from the Bishop of Bristol, who is seeking you everywhere, as his Lordship wishes to see you on particular business?" Beverley thanked him for his information, and hastened to Trinity, Jemmy following him at no great distance. "I understand you are wishing to see me, my Lord," said Beverley, addressing the Bishop; to which the latter replied, "You have been misinformed, Mr Beverley". At that moment

---

* Æschines in Ctesiph. Pag. 447.

Jemmy joined them, and taking off his hat most respectfully, said, "I think, my Lord, I am entitled to the half-crown!" The next time the Bishop met Jemmy, he took an opportunity of proving to him that there was *no great difference* of opinion between them respecting Mr Beverley.

For many years this extraordinary character infested the streets, swearing and blaspheming in the most horrible manner; the magistrates not interfering, from a reluctance to expose themselves to his violent and abusive language. At length the nuisance became intolerable, and Jemmy usually passed nine or ten weeks of every quarter in the Town Gaol. It was during one of these incarcerations, that John Taylor, the University Marshal, consulted me respecting a letter he had received from a person formerly a member of the University, in which he was asked to go to Maps (a well-known character) and request him to procure for him short essays in Latin, on six subjects which he sent him, all of a serious and religious nature. As Maps was dead, Taylor was at a loss how to proceed, and wished to know who was his successor. I told him I believed there was no one in that line now; but added, jocularly, that I thought Jemmy Gordon would supply them. Jemmy was then in gaol, and as he had been there for a long time, was, of necessity, sober. The same evening Taylor called upon me, and showed me an essay on one of the subjects; he asked my opinion of it: (it occupied three sides of a sheet of foolscap): I told him there was no objection to it but its length, and that if Gordon would reduce it to one-third of its size, and observe the same rule with the other five, I thought they would answer his friend's purpose very well. They were finished in the course of that night and the following day, and Jemmy received a half a guinea for each, which Taylor learned, from some quarter or other, was the price usually given for works of that description. But these opportunities of obtaining money during imprisonment, seldom occurred, and by constant importunity he had wearied out those persons who, having known him in his better days, were unwilling that he should suffer from want. The instant he was released, and had begged a little money, he repeated that outrageous conduct which it was disgraceful to the magistracy to have so long tolerated, and which was loudly censured by all persons visiting the University. The fact was, that the characters of the magistrates at that time were not invulnerable: they possessed, at least, a proportionate share of the failings of their fellow-citizens, and were afraid that Jemmy (who was no respector of persons) should proclaim, from the Huntingdon turnpike to Addenbrooke's Hospital, their frailties in his loudest tones. It was therefore arranged between the magistrates and Jemmy, that he should leave Cambridge, never to return.

He betook himself to London, and was to be seen daily waiting the arrival or departure of the Cambridge coaches: in this manner he earned a precarious subsistence; for even in London he became notorious, and is described at some length in one of Bulwer's early novels. The London police, however, had no sympathy with Jemmy; when he offended against the laws he was taken to prison, where he had nothing to look to but the prison allowance. Jemmy sighed for liberty and his native air, and at last found his way back to Cambridge, where he lived in a state of the greatest destitution. For many months he slept in the grove belonging to Jesus College, where he conveyed a bundle of straw which was but seldom changed. When winter set in, he was allowed to sleep in the straw-chamber belonging to the Hoop Hotel; still, on receiving a few shillings, he squandered them in the usual manner; offended and disgusted every one he met with; and when he became sober, often found himself in prison. In ascending his usual resting-place one night, when he was very drunk, he slipped off the ladder and broke his thigh; he called loudly for assistance; the ostler and post-boys, not believing he had received any injury, took him up and threw him into an adjoining outhouse for the night: when in the morning he was found to be incapable of moving, he was taken on a shutter to the hospital; but was in so filthy a condition that he was refused admittance; he was then taken to the workhouse at Barnwell, where he died, after several weeks of suffering.

JOHN NICHOLSON ("MAPS")

An equally well-known character in the University, but of a far different stamp, was a bookseller, who was universally known by the name of *Maps*, though his only son, to whom he left a handsome property, discovered he was entitled to the name of Nicholson. When he first began business, he was a seller of maps and pictures, which he exhibited in the streets on a small movable stall; but when I came to college he was living in an old-fashioned, but large and commodious house belonging to King's College, and adjoining to what was then the Provost's Lodge. He had a very large stock of books required at college lectures, both classical and mathematical; and I do not believe I expended, during my undergraduateship, twenty shillings in the purchase of books for the lecture-room. His terms of subscription were five shillings and threepence per quarter, but were afterwards increased to seven shillings and sixpence. When his house was pulled down to make way for the Screen which connects the Chapel of King's with the New Building, he built and removed to the house now occupied by Macmillan. He was indefatigable in pursuit of business, and was to be seen most part

Vol. I, pp.181–182

of the day loaded with books, going from room to room in the different colleges, and announcing himself by shouting MAPS as he proceeded. Persons requiring themes, or declamations, or compositions on occasional subjects, were in the habit of applying to him, and if they had no objection to pay a high price, were furnished with articles of considerable literary merit. It was said that manuscript sermons might be obtained through him; but in every transaction of this kind he strictly concealed the names of the parties concerned. By the desire of Dr Farmer, his truly characteristic portrait was placed on the staircase of the Public Library, a distinction he was better entitled to, than a *smirking Professor* in scarlet robes, who hangs very near him.

Dr Richard Watson
Bishop of Llandaff

Vol. I,
pp.212–
215

Richard Watson, of Trinity, took his B.A. degree as second Wrangler in 1759, and M.A. 1762. He was Tutor of Trinity, and Professor of Chemistry: he obtained the appointment of Regius Professor of Divinity in 1771, and became Bishop of Llandaff in 1782.

The ill state of his health rendering his manifold duties too heavy for him, he was allowed to appoint a deputy in his professorship, and Dr Kipling undertook the office at a salary of two hundred pounds per annum. There was much dissatisfaction at the time of the appointment, and after the Bishop had determined on leaving Cambridgeshire and building a house on the banks of Windermere, many attempts were made to compel him to resign his professorship in the University, and as a matter of course, the Church preferments connected with it. Several Graces were brought forward for this purpose by Burden of Emmanuel, who (judging from the perseverance with which he agitated the question) was supposed to have had a personal dislike to Watson. It was however generally understood that the electors alone possessed the power of enforcing residence, and as THEY had allowed him to appoint a deputy, the Senate could not interfere.

The beauties of Westmorland were at this time but little known. The Bishop built an excellent house, and occupied much of his leisure time with the cultivation of land. He attended regularly in the House of Lords for many years, and when passing through Cambridge, occasionally dined with the Vice-Chancellor. He frequently spoke in high terms of his new residence, and remarked how much the face of the neighbourhood was improved by his numerous plantations, for which he had obtained several medals.

A ludicrous anecdote just occurs to me; and as the Bishop related it with as much mirth as his companions received it, I am tempted to give the story a place in my Reminiscences.

The principal inn at the head of Windermere had been known as the Cock; but the landlord, by way of compliment to his distinguished neighbour, substituted the *Bishop* as the new sign. An inn-keeper close by, who had frequently envied mine host of the Cock for his good fortune in securing a considerable preponderance of visitors, took advantage of the change, and attracted many travellers to his house by putting up the sign of the Cock. The landlord with the new sign was much discomfited at seeing many of his old customers deposited at his rival's establishment; so by way of remedy, he put up in large red letters, under the portrait of the Bishop, "THIS IS THE OLD COCK"!

During one of the Bishop's short residences, I accidentally met him one morning in Trinity walks, and we had much conversation. The principal topic (and at that period the all-absorbing one) was Burke's publication, of which I have previously made mention. The Bishop remarked, it contained an allusion which none seemed to understand, but that his opinion of the accuracy and extent of Burke's knowledge was such, that he had made a bet with a friend that Burke was right, and that he had undertaken to prove it. The words were: "This circumstance was as well known as the Systasis of Crete, or the Confederation of Poland". He confessed that he had been making an unsuccessful search for "the Systasis of Crete", in several volumes in the University Library, and he requested me to inquire among my friends and report to him, if I could obtain any information. Among others I applied to Ramsden, who thought he had discovered the passage Burke must have had in his mind at the time. Aristotle, in his work *Peripolitia*, uses the expression *Sustantes tinas*; but certainly these words did not speak of a transaction of such a public nature as to justify Burke's application of the term. I never learned whether the Bishop was able to satisfy himself on the subject.

Dr Samuel Ogden
Woodwardian Professor of Geology

Amongst the very eccentric characters of the University was Samuel Ogden. He took his B.A. degree in 1737, and that of D.D. in 1753. He was elected Professor of Geology in 1764. Ogden was a man of good property; and although in many instances very penurious, yet he was remarkably fond of good living, and had upon one occasion characterized the goose as a silly bird—too much for one, and not enough for two. He would dine out whenever he had an opportunity, but pleaded his age and infirmities for asking no one in return.

Vol. 1, pp. 215–219

When my father was in college, he frequently went to see the Doctor on a Sunday afternoon, and

took coffee with him. Invariably the first question
was, "Hast any news to tell?" Upon one occasion
my father replied, "I have just heard that Dr ——
is dead". "Art sure?—what's thy authority?"
My father replied, he had heard it from James
Bullman, the scholars' butler. "Shabby authority;
go and try if thou canst not mend it!" On my
father's return, he said he had by chance met the
confidential servant of the deceased, who had confirmed the news. "That will do," said he, "and
now let me see. He had a stall at Canterbury, and
two livings, all in the gift of the Crown—let's try
what we can lay our hands upon—take a pen, and
write as I dictate." He dictated as follows: "The
great are always liable to importunity; those who
are both good and great are liable to a double portion". I have frequently heard my father repeat
the rest of the letter, but I can only call to mind the
two short sentences with which it began; the remaining part was written in the same peculiar style,
and was addressed to the Prime Minister. However, he was always unsuccessful in his applications
for preferment. It was only his reputed wealth that
made him a *produceable* man, for he was singularly
uncouth in his manner, and spoke his mind very
freely upon all occasions.

A very characteristic anecdote just occurs to me.
The Doctor had taken a great fancy to a lad who
had been in his service three or four years; he was

much pleased with his management of a garden which was attached to his house, and of which he was particularly fond. A cherry-tree, which had been planted some time, and which should have produced very choice fruit, had constantly failed. To the Doctor's great delight, it at last showed signs of bearing, and about a dozen cherries after a while began to assume a tempting appearance. Returning one day from his ride, he missed some of his cherries, and accused the boy of having taken them. "I have not touched them," replied the boy, "as true as God's in heaven"—(a very common mode of assertion among inferior people at that time). "That's a good lad! sit thee down, and I'll give thee a glass of wine, for thou wouldst not tell me a lie!" Going to his closet, he put a pretty strong dose of antimonial wine into a glass, which the boy drank off, and was preparing to leave the room, but his master kept him in conversation. At length the boy was making a *hasty retreat*, saying he did not feel well. "Do not quit the room," said the Doctor, "sit thee down; thou wilt soon be better"; and ringing the bell, ordered a jug of warm water, which he administered very freely, at the same time providing a basin. The cherries soon made their appearance—to the great consternation of the lad. "Where's the God in heaven?" said the Doctor. "Thou miscreant! get thee out of my house!" He quitted it the same day, but not until the Doctor had showed him his will, in which he had left him 200*l.* This person was many years afterwards my bedmaker at College: a more honest man never breathed, but he was addicted to drinking. I could not help pitying the poor fellow, for he never recovered the shock he received when listening to the Doctor's bequest; in fact, he never seemed altogether in his right mind whilst he was in my service.

When the Doctor was dining one day with the High Steward at Wimpole, to meet many of the Heads of colleges, and where a most sumptuous dinner was provided, Lord Hardwicke ordered champagne (which was very uncommon in those days) to be handed round. On a glass being taken to his Lordship, he immediately perceived that the butler had drawn a bottle of pale brandy, and he discovered, to his utter astonishment, that the Doctor, who sat on his right, had emptied his glass. His Lordship expressed surprise that he had not noticed the mistake; to which the Doctor replied, "I did not remark it to you, my lord, because I felt it my duty to take whatever you thought proper to offer me, if not with pleasure, at least in silence!"

Upon another occasion, when the mistress of the house asked him his opinion of a dish of ruffs and reeves (which were *rather under-done*), he replied "They are admirable, Madam—*raw*; what must they have been had they been roasted!"

From the singularity of Dr Ogden's manner, as

well as of his matter, he was very popular in the
pulpit: he preached at the Round Church, which
was always crowded. His successor in the parish
was Dr Hallifax, who affected his tone and manner
of delivery, but did not succeed in attracting so
numerous a congregation.

Dr Lowther Yates
Master of St Catharine's College

During the Vice-Chancellorship of Dr Yates, a circumstance occurred which, had it not been for the
extreme good nature of the Vice-Chancellor, might
have been attended with very unpleasant conse-
quences to the principal actor in it. In order that
the matter may be understood, it is necessary to
say a few words respecting the figure of the Vice-
Chancellor. He was low in stature, remarkably fat,
his form was spherical, and his legs extremely short
and thick: he appeared to a person following him
not very unlike a turtle walking on his hind legs. I
was accompanying him to St Mary's on a Saint's
day, when I heard the sound of a very jovial party
breakfasting on King's Parade. One of them looking out of the window saw us approach; and before
we got opposite the house, they all joined in a very
loud and noisy song, of which the following words
could be very distinctly heard:

*Vol. II,
pp. 6–9*

> What is't I see? Gadzoons! gadzoons!
> Lowther Yates in pantaloons!

These words were often repeated. The Vice-Chancellor directed me to cross the street; and on Mrs Perry coming to the door, he demanded to see the lodger who was giving the entertainment. Charles Valentine Le Grice, of Trinity, made his appearance. The Vice-Chancellor, highly excited, asked what he meant by insulting him; to this he replied, that there was not the most distant idea of insulting him, but that as they were singing, *somehow or other* his name slipped into the song. We then left him and went to St Mary's, having ascertained his name and college. As soon as I had left the Vice-Chancellor at his Lodge, I called upon Le Grice, with whom I had a slight acquaintance; I urged him to wait upon the Vice-Chancellor immediately, and to make the best apology in his power for the insult of which he had been guilty. He followed my advice, and found the Vice-Chancellor at first too angry to listen to any excuse; but by degrees he softened, and said, "If I were to forgive you, Sir, the story would be all over the University before the evening". "True," replied Le Grice; "but the story of your clemency would accompany it wherever it went!" The kind-hearted old man forgave him. The words were subsequently set to music by the Catch and Glee Club at Huntingdon, where I heard them regularly sung; and if the Club still exist, I have no doubt it remains on their books, although few of their members are aware of its origin.

Shortly after this, I was attending Dr Yates one Sunday morning to St Mary's. We saw on the opposite side of the street a gentleman in military uniform, accompanied by an undergraduate, proceeding in a contrary direction to ourselves. The Vice-Chancellor called across the street in a loud tone, "Why are you not going to St Mary's?" *In those days,* to have answered that he was going to another church would have been a great aggravation of his offence, as our statutes denounce severely all persons *in statu pupillari* attending any other than St Mary's. The undergraduate stopped for a few seconds, stared hard at Dr Yates, and walked on without making any reply. *John Taylor* was despatched to learn his name, and brought word that it was Francis Bedingfield, of St John's. A meeting of the Heads was called, and Mr Bedingfield was summoned to attend it. I was also summoned as a witness. I stated the circumstances as I have related them above, and was about to leave the room, when one of the Heads called me back, and asked whether, in my opinion, the conduct of Mr Bedingfield was not disrespectful and insolent to the Vice-Chancellor? I replied that I had stated the facts accurately, but that I must decline to give an opinion on a subject upon which I might probably be mistaken. I added, that the Vice-Chancellor had witnessed everything, and was the proper person to tell them what impression the circumstances had made on his mind. I was then permitted to retire, although there was much whispering among the Heads, and I judged that several were dissatisfied with my answer. It appeared that the officer in company with the undergraduate was his uncle; he had breakfasted with his nephew at St John's, and was going to his inn, in order to post to his brother's seat in Suffolk. I do not at this distant period precisely remember the result, but I think the punishment was but slight.

WILLIAM PUGH
Fellow of Trinity College

*Vol. II,
pp.* 53–
56
William Pugh, of Trinity, took his B.A. degree in 1789, and that of M.A. in 1792. He was a man of unsocial habits, very slovenly, and altogether unprepossessing in his appearance; but he possessed considerable talent, and devoted most of his time to reading. I heard him keep his Act, in which he displayed extraordinary learning, but no great knowledge of the subjects under discussion; hence he considered that Hailstone had conferred on him a very appropriate honour when, after complimenting him on the composition of his thesis, he added, "*Erudite disputasti*".

Pugh's name did not appear on the Tripos, probably on account of ill health; but he was elected Fellow of the Society, and it was understood he had passed a remarkably good examination.

When he took his B.D. degree, he read a very long, a very learned, and eccentric thesis, which was entirely written on the covers of letters.

Soon after he became Fellow, he was applied to by Dr Farmer to make a catalogue of the books in the University Library, for which his acquaintance with various languages, and his habits of intense application, particularly qualified him. He almost lived in the Library, and so absorbed did he appear in his occupation that he occasionally forgot his dinner.

The Librarian, from time to time, advanced him money on account without hesitation, not doubting but that he had earned more than he applied for. At length Dr Farmer expressed a wish to see what progress he had made in the catalogue, when he discovered to his great astonishment that very little had been done; and no wonder, for it appeared, whenever he came to a work with which he was unacquainted, he was not content with looking at the title-page, but applied himself to reading its contents. Had he been paid according to the time he was shut up in the library, a good deal would have been due to him; but for the little he had done, he was considerably overpaid. In consequence of his small progress in the work he had undertaken, he was given to understand that his services were no longer required. This had such an effect upon him (for he was as passionately fond of money as he was

of books) that he became frantic. On the evening
he received his dismissal, he sallied into the streets
with a long stick in his hand, breaking the lamps
as he proceeded. Whenever he smashed one, he exclaimed, "Death to the villain Marat! destruction
to Robespierre!"

As there were no police at this time, he continued
his work of demolition until Trinity and Trumpington streets were in darkness. He was at length secured and taken back to college, whence he was
afterwards removed and placed under restraint,
and for several years he was lost to the University.

On his return (though his manners were extremely
eccentric) he was quiet and inoffensive. When called
upon to take part in the college examinations for
scholarships and fellowships, he particularly distinguished himself; and I have been told upon un-
questionable authority, that provided the merits
of the candidates were nearly equal, Pugh was
more competent than any other man to decide.

His society was sought by many to whom his
reputed wealth was a bait; but he made a point of
leaving no part of it to those who had been most
attentive to him. To Musgrave he left several acres
of land; and the property arising from the emolu-
ments of his vicarage he left for the benefit of the
parish, taking effectual care to exclude from the
management of it the Rev. George Jenyns, who
was the principal man in it, but to whom Pugh had

taken a singular dislike. He considered all provincial banks insecure; yet when he died several hundred pounds of Mortlock's notes were found in his pockets, many of which appeared as if they had been there for years.

Section iv

MISCELLANEOUS

STOURBRIDGE FAIR

Vol. I,
*pp.*148–
158.
1789 ON THE 18TH OF SEPTEMBER, THE CERE-
mony of proclaiming Stourbridge Fair took place.
At 11 A.M., the Vice-Chancellor, with the Bedells
and Registrary, the Commissary, the Proctors, and
the Taxors, attended in the Senate House, where a
plentiful supply of mulled wine and sherry, in
black bottles, with a great variety of cakes, awaited
their arrival. Strange as it may seem, the company
partook of these things as heartily as if they had
come without their breakfasts, or were apprehensive of going without their dinners. This important
business ended, the parties proceeded to the Fair,
in carriages provided for the occasion. The procla-
mation was read by the Registrary in the carriage
with the Vice-Chancellor, and repeated by the
Yeoman Bedell on horseback, in three different
places. At the conclusion of this ceremony, the
carriages drew up to the *Tiled Booth* (which is still
standing), where the company alighted for the
dispatch of business—and of oysters; and passing
through an upper room, which was crowded by a
motley assemblage of customers, most of whom
had been there from an early hour, they at length
arrived at what was called "The University Dining

Room ". This consisted of a slip of a room, separated
from the other part by a wooden partition, made of
the rudest materials, which was about six feet and
a half high, with two doors in it. Close to the end
wall was a narrow bench; next that, the table,
formed from rough materials, and supported by
tressels and casks; on this table (which had no
cloth of any kind) were placed several barrels of
oysters, with ale and bottled porter in great profusion. At this repast we were joined by numbers of
Masters of Arts, who had formed no part of the
procession, but who had come for the express purpose of eating oysters. This was *a very serious part*
of the day's proceedings, and occupied a long time.
We then left the *dining-room,* that the waiters
might remove the shells and cover the boards with
a cloth, in preparation for dinner. That part of the
room not appropriated to the University was by
this time crowded almost to suffocation, and we
had some trouble in getting to the open air. We
took two or three turns in Garlick-row, and then
returned to the *Tiled Booth*; but to reach the
dining-room was a very arduous task. In vain did
the Marshal, the Yeoman Bedell, the Proctors' and
Taxors' men, attempt to form a lane through
which we might pass without obstruction; in vain
did the landlord of the *Tiled Booth* shout out,
"Make way for the Vice-Chancellor and the University !" Not a man made an attempt to stir; for with

the peasantry (who on this day formed the majority
of the company assembled) the University was
highly unpopular; they seemed to enjoy the difficulties we had to encounter. Nor was it to be
wondered at, for they had heard it *solemnly proclaimed* that every man would be punished who
sold beer in any other mug than such as were
allowed by the University; and as the mugs out of
which they were then drinking were shamefully
under the standard measure, they suspected that the
dinner, of which we were about to partake, was paid
for with their money. Of these suspicions the pub-
licans took no means to disabuse them; indeed,
many of those who sold beer *actually believed* that
the money they paid at the Commissary's Court
was for a permission to sell short measure. At
length, by a perseverance worthy of a better cause,
we reached the dining-room. The cloth had been
laid, and the dinner served up as soon as we had
quitted it; and as *covers* were unknown at the *Tiled
Booth,* the joints would have been cold, if anything
could have been cold in a climate intolerable even to
a native of the tropics. The scene which presented
itself on entering the room I can describe most accurately, for the dishes and their arrangement
never varied. Before the Vice-Chancellor was
placed a large dish of herrings; then followed in
order a neck of pork roasted, an enormous plum-
pudding, a leg of pork boiled, a pease-pudding, a

goose, a huge apple-pie, and a round of beef in the centre. On the other half of the table, the same dishes were placed in similar order (the herrings before the Senior Proctor, who sat at the bottom). From thirty to forty persons dined there; and although the wine was execrable, a number of toasts were given, and mirth and good humour prevailed, to such an extent as is seldom to be met with at more modern and more refined entertainments. At about half-past six the dinner party broke up, and with scarcely an exception, adjourned to the theatre. Previously to this, however, a day (usually the 24th) was fixed for holding the Commissary's Court, and for repeating the oyster-eating and dining I have just described.

The Corporation proclaimed the fair*, and had their dinner also; but it possessed this advantage over ours, that it was given at a private house, where they were served with an abundance of venison and game, which at that time (as they could not be purchased) were considered great luxuries.

At this distance of time, it seems to me quite unaccountable that Fellows of colleges, in the humblest of whose halls a clean and comfortable repast was provided, should sit down a second time at such a table as I have described.

* In 1790, the procession of the Corporation was discontinued, and the fair was proclaimed by the Mayor, Bailiffs, and Town Clerk only.

In the year 1803, a cousin of mine (a Fellow of
King's) was Senior Proctor, and resolved, with the
consent of his colleague, to transfer the dinner from
the *Tiled Booth* at the fair to the Rose Tavern at
Cambridge. He took care that the Commissary's
Court should be held at the accustomed place, and
made ample provision for the lovers of ale and
oysters; he also gave a fortnight's notice of his in-
tentions, and sent a courteous note to each of the
officials, containing an invitation to dinner. The
Commissary (Dr Fisher) returned an angry and
elaborate answer, in which the *right* of the Proctor
to alter the place of dining was called in question,
and he was accused of violating the "Consuetu-
dines approbatas", which he had sworn to
defend, &c. &c.!

The Commissary gave the dinner as usual at the
Tiled Booth, at his own expense, brought old members of the University from a distance of thirty
miles to dine with him, and by a personal canvass
prevailed on most of the officials to be of his party.
He had a complete triumph, and sat at the head of
a crowded table, whilst the Proctor could muster
no more than eight or ten to sanction his bold in-
novation. Subsequent Proctors and Taxors were
well pleased to get rid of the expense, and gave up
the dinner at the Rose, and the Commissary after
a time discontinued the dinner at the *Tiled Booth*.
The Commissary's Court is still held, but the re-

ceipts are very trifling; and oysters and ale are still
provided for those who choose to partake of them.

Stourbridge Fair was, at the time I am now
speaking of, a place of considerable importance,
not only on account of the various trades that were
carried on there, but as furnishing sights and
scenes rarely to be met with out of the metropolis.
I will endeavour to describe it, and I trust my
memory will enable me to do so pretty accurately.
As soon as you left Barnwell, there was a small
public-house on the right-hand side, called the
Race-horse; here the cheese fair began; from thence
till you came opposite the road leading to Chesterton Ferry, the ground was exclusively occupied by
dealers in that article. It was the great mart at
which all the dealers in cheese from Cottenham,
Willingham, with other villages in the county and
isle assembled; there were also traders from Leices-
tershire, Derbyshire, Cheshire, and Gloucestershire.
Not only did the inhabitants of the neighbouring
counties supply themselves with their annual stock
of cheese, but great quantities were bought and
sent up to London, the practice of employing
travellers being at that time scarcely known. In
the neighbourhood of the Chapel, which is still
standing (1851), there were about a dozen booths,
called "Ironmongers Row": these, among a great
variety of other articles, furnished the goods required by saddlers and harness-makers, together

with every description of leather in great abundance. One of the proprietors I perfectly recollect; his name was Rose, he resided in London, where he carried on a very extensive business. During the three weeks the fair lasted, he lodged at Cambridge, and went to his booth every morning after breakfast, returning to a late dinner; he lived in a good style, kept a handsome chariot, drove a pair of very fine horses, and his servants' liveries were as handsome as those of any gentleman in the county.

Another row of booths, reaching from the Chapel to Paper Mills turnpike, was called "The Duddery". These contained woollen cloths from Yorkshire and the western counties of England; but this part of the fair was beginning to be on the decline. There was also a very large piece of ground set apart for the sale of hops. A considerable part of the Common was occupied by earthenware and china from the Potteries, and by the coarser wares from Ely. On the left-hand side of the road, leading from the Newmarket road to the Ferry, was a row of booths extending to the Common; they consisted of silk-mercers, linendrapers, furriers, stationers, an immense variety of toys, and also of musical instruments. At one of these booths, I recollect that if you bought an instrument, the proprietor undertook to give lessons upon it gratis. The most conspicuous person in the fair (and whose booth stood upon three times as much ground as the largest amongst them) was named Green; he came from Limehouse, and dealt in tea, sugar, soap, candles, and every other article in grocery that housekeepers could possibly require. His goods were of the first quality, and he sold them as cheap as they could be bought in London; so that any family in Cambridge, or within thirty miles of it (who could afford the money), laid in their annual stock at that season. He was also an extensive dealer in pickles. This man was a widower, with one daughter, who always accompanied her father. She was, at the age of fourteen, very pretty, and was called by the University men, who stopped *to admire her father's pickles*, "Miss Gherkin"; she grew, however, so very large, that the name of Gherkin (or of "Little Pickle") could no longer be applied to her with any propriety, and she was then styled "Miss Mango". There was not the slightest vulgarity in her manner or conversation, and it was remarked by an incorrigible punster (of St John's) that she was *Wapping* in nothing but her size. This young lady was a decided coquette, and many members of the University, of *various ages* and *various ranks*, were in the habit of paying her much attention. Her father was extremely proud of the admiration she excited, and wished it to be understood that "the man of her choice would find he had not made a very bad bargain". What became of her I know not, but it was to me rather unaccountable that so rich a prize (whose conduct was without reproach) should visit Cambridge for eight or ten years without getting a husband.

Besides the tradesmen, there was the usual mixture of dwarfs and giants, conjurors and learned pigs. It was a common practice for some of us who were well acquainted with the University, to enter into a confederacy with these conjurors, and with the owners of these learned animals, to give them a string of questions and answers, and to point out some mode by which they might discover the persons to whom the answers were particularly applicable. In consequence of this secret intelligence, the characters of the conjurors and the pigs stood higher at Stourbridge Fair than at any other place. Persons guilty of indiscretions, which they flattered themselves were known only to their most intimate friends, were astonished at finding that the sapient pig was acquainted with their proceedings, and pointed them out with but little hesitation to the assembled crowd.

There were a great number of drinking-booths. One was on a very large scale, over the doors of which was painted, "Quod petis hic est". In this booth (if the weather was fine) men from the country, with their wives and families, used to feast on geese, pork, and herrings, luxuries that were to be had in great abundance, and which were served to perfection.

There was a theatre on the spot where the
Shakspeare public-house now stands; it belonged
to the Norwich company, which generally com-
prised many respectable, and frequently very excellent performers. Brunton was for many years
manager. His performance of Shylock and Iago
was highly applauded; his daughter and several of
his relations were much distinguished on the London boards. The performances continued for about
three weeks; the house was generally well filled,
and on some evenings crowded in every part, especially when the Lord Lieutenant, or the members of the town and University, bespoke the play.
Dr Farmer never failed to be present, except on
Michaelmas-day, which was the anniversary of the
foundation of Emmanuel, and which was always
celebrated by a splendid dinner in the college hall.
On every other evening he with his friends, George
Stevens, Isaac Reed, Malone, and one or two
others (whom Dr Barnes used to designate the
Shakspeare Gang), were accustomed to occupy that
part of the pit which is usually called "The
Critic's Row", and which was scrupulously reserved for them. They seemed to enjoy the play as
much as the youngest persons present. They were
the best-natured and most indulgent of critics; and
as these dramatic enthusiasts never expressed dis-
approbation, few other persons ventured to do
so; but when they approved, the whole house

applauded most rapturously. Dr Farmer and his
friends rarely left before the whole performance was
concluded; the party joined loudly in the mirth
which the fairies of those days never failed to produce, in the midst of which the hearty and very
peculiar laugh of the Doctor could easily be distinguished. When the performance was over, they
returned on foot, and adjourned to *Emmanuel
Parlour*, where half-a-score persons were either
waiting for them, or accompanied them home.

Bourn Bridge

Vol. I,
pp. 223–
226

For many years after I came to the University,
the County Balls were held at Bourn Bridge, where
there were some large rooms well adapted for the
purpose. All the families of distinction in the county
made a point of attending: the county of Suffolk
contributing very largely. The town of Bury also
furnished its quota of beautiful women, for which
it was at that time highly distinguished. There were
also held at the same place, archery meetings at
which prizes were given. One of the most skilful of
the toxophilites was Norcross of Pembroke, who
generally carried away the silver arrow, though he
had to contend with bowmen from distant counties,
archery being at that time a favourite amusement
of the English gentry. Marquees were pitched in
the adjoining grounds, where the contest took

place, and refreshments were dealt out with a most liberal hand.

But it may be observed that in those days the company did not present that promiscuous assemblage which the experience of modern times might lead us to expect. The distinction between different ranks was strictly observed, hence no police was necessary to keep off intruders. Persons of inferior condition were prevented by their own sense of propriety from intruding, and were but too happy in viewing from the turnpike-road, the sports in which the gentry were engaged.

In the evening a dinner was given to a party of seventy or eighty persons of both sexes, by the members of the different clubs assembled, to which no persons were admitted but by invitation. After the prizes were distributed, whist and guadrille (*quadrilles* not having then been heard of) kept the company together till a very late hour.

At Bourn Bridge the various clubs belonging to the University held their dinners. On one of these occasions the following remarkable circumstance took place. A gentleman of the party drank so freely during dinner, that very soon after the cloth was removed he became extremely troublesome. The chairman remonstrated with him frequently, but to no purpose. At length the company, who had by that time taken a considerable quantity of wine, determined to abate the nuisance. They therefore seized him by the legs and arms, and carried him out of the room with as little ceremony as a policeman would use in conveying a "disorderly" to a police-station. They put him into a bed-room, and throwing him on the bed, left the room, locking the door and taking the key away.

Being unable to force the door, and nobody attending to his calls, he formed the desperate resolution of throwing himself out of the window. Some of the company, who were seated opposite the windows, saw him fall; they immediately ran down, expecting to find him a corpse. To their utter surprise, not a bone was broken, nor did he complain of being hurt. Some of the party offered him a bet that he dare not take that leap again, whilst others invited him to resume his seat at the table. He was much too angry, however, to accede to either proposal, but, ordering a chaise, returned to college in great dudgeon. I was not acquainted with him, but I understood that he was very slightly hurt, and did not even call in a surgeon. The height from which he fell I do not know, but it must have been upwards of thirty feet, and upon a hard gravel road. Between thirty and forty years after this event I met Lord Lyndhurst at dinner, and one of the persons present related the circumstance, and asked his lordship if he remembered it, to which he replied, "Perfectly, and, if I mistake not", he added, "I was one of the party".

On the opposite side of the road was another inn, not so splendid as that I have been describing, but affording excellent "accommodation for man and horse", particularly for the latter, as there was a very large dog-kennel fitted for the accommodation of a pack of fox-hounds, which was kept there for several weeks in the season.

It so happened, however, that the Excise officers made a very large seizure of tea which was concealed in the kennel; after which it became, and continued for several years, a private house; it was afterwards pulled down, and the larger inn reduced to its present dimensions. For some time this latter continued to let post horses, but that business is, I suspect, put a stop to by the railway.

WILLIAM V
Prince of Orange

During Milner's first or second Vice-Chancellor-ship (I don't recollect which) the Stadtholder came to Cambridge. The Vice-Chancellor and the Heads waited upon him at the Rose, attended him to St Mary's Church, and accompanied him back to his inn. When we were all assembled at the Rose, the Stadtholder unfortunately asked whence the text was taken. As we were none of us very clear on that subject, we held our tongues, but Beverley, with his usual intrepidity, answered, "It was from the Second Epistle of Jude": "There is but one

Vol. I, *p.* 248

Epistle," said the Stadtholder.—"Certainly not," said Beverley, "I intended to have said the second chapter!"—"Unfortunately", said his Serene Highness, "there is but one chapter!" Beverley's mistakes quickly spread through the University, and were set to music by some member of the Huntingdonshire Catch-Club. The words were as follows:

> Fie, Beverley, fie: your Biblical lie
> Was vastly too forward and rude;
> For the future be shy, nor dare to reply,
> But remember the Second of Jude!

Vol. II, pp. 63–64. 1797

In the spring of this year, the Stadtholder made a second visit to Cambridge, and the Vice-Chancellor and Heads went to pay their respects to him on the Sunday morning at the Rose Inn. Having previously assembled at Caius Lodge, the Vice-Chancellor expressed a doubt as to the title by which the Prince should be addressed. Mr Beverley, with his usual promptness, replied, "His *Royal* Highness, without doubt". Dr Belward then asked me. I answered, "I believe *Serene* Highness is his proper title". On being pressed to give a reason for thinking so, I was obliged to confess that I had no other reason than the recollection of a caricature I had seen in St James's Street (when in town the previous week), in which the Prince was represented *as a very fat pig*, standing on his hind legs *fast asleep*, under which was written, "His *Serene* Highness".

Dr Belward, who was a very solemn man, was not at all satisfied with the reason, and observed that his was a serious question, and ought to have received a serious answer. Probably on this account he declined to invite me to supper, when a large party of the University assembled to meet his *Serene Highness*. I am therefore not enabled, from my own knowledge, to state what took place in the course of the evening; but I was told that when the healths of the King and Royal Family were drunk the Prince responded, observing that he considered himself one of that family.

To this they all assented, adding that few kings in history could boast of so numerous a family. He said that King Jacob (which he pronounced I-a-cob) had a much more numerous family: to this they also assented.

At length, emboldened by the recollection of Beverley's *Second of Jude*, he examined them as to the number of which that family consisted, and receiving a variety of answers, exclaimed in a triumphant tone, "You are all mistaken; I-a-cob's family consisted of threescore and ten persons".

THE MIDLENT SUNDAY SERMON AT BURWELL

It was on Midlent Sunday of this year that I received a very early message by the University Marshal to accompany the Vice-Chancellor to Burwell, my colleague, Beverley, reporting himself as *Vol. II, pp. 10–12. 1795* having been taken suddenly ill. It has been the custom for many years for the Vice-Chancellor to preach a sermon at Burwell on Midlent Sunday, and to dine with the tenant. The University is possessed of a considerable estate there, consisting of the glebe lands and the great tithes of the parish; they are also patrons of the Vicarage.

On the night previous to my being summoned a very heavy snow had fallen; but notwithstanding this (added to the execrable state of the roads), the villages of Bottisham and Swaffham were crowded with people, who did not in those days scruple to come from a distance to see a "coach and four". The Marshal, who had filled his pockets with half-pence for the occasion, amused himself with throwing them into the snow, and we laughed heartily to see the scramble for them.

When we arrived at the Devil's Ditch, two strong cart-horses and their driver (belonging to the tenant) were in waiting, and we had several spare traces in the carriage. At this point we quitted the road altogether, and went across the ploughed lands. There was no longer any danger of over-turning, but the six horses were obliged to exert themselves to the utmost to keep the carriage in motion. At length we arrived at the vicarage, where we stopped and had some refreshment; and then proceeded to the church, a very noble edifice, and filled almost to suffocation by persons who had

come (notwithstanding the badness of the day) to
see a Vice-Chancellor. After the sermon we proceeded to the old Manor House, situated about
three-quarters of a mile from the church, and on the
very edge of the Fens. We were conducted into a
small parlour, and in a few minutes were told that
dinner was on the table. The repast was of the
most ample description; three huge fowls were at
the top of the table; at the bottom was an enormous sirloin of beef; on one side, a huge ham of
excellent flavour; on the other side, a pigeon-pie;
and in the centre, an unusually large plum-pudding.
The only guests in the upper chamber consisted of
the Vice-Chancellor, Mr Turner (the Vicar), myself, and Mr Dunn, the tenant. The beer was excellent. After dinner, wine was introduced; the port
was as good as ever was tasted, and the tenant
circulated the bottle very briskly. I confess that I
did not consider the Clerk, who came to say he
was going to chime, a welcome visitor; and the
Sexton, who came about a quarter of an hour afterwards to say the bells were ringing, was, I believe,
very unwelcome to us all. We got into the carriage
(which was ordered to wait for us at the gate) and
went to church, where the Vicar read the prayers.
The excellence of the tenant's ale was apparent,
not only in the red faces of the Vicar, the Clerk,
and the Sexton, but also in the vigour with which
two or three officials, furnished with white staves,

exercised them whenever they found any of the
children inattentive. Not contented with showing
their authority over the younger part of the congregation, one of them inflicted so heavy a blow on the
head of a young man who was sleeping, that it re-
sounded through the church. The person thus distinguished started up, and rubbing his head, had
the mortification to find all his neighbours laughing
at his expense; to use a fancy phrase, "he showed
fight", and I believe he was only restrained by the
presence of the Vice-Chancellor (who rose to see
what was the matter) from giving the peace-officer
a hearty drubbing.

We had rather a perilous journey back to Cambridge, being very nearly upset before we reached
the high road.

Vol. II,
*pp.*160–
163.
1801

On Midlent Sunday in this year, according to
annual custom, the Vice-Chancellor (Dr Gretton),
accompanied by the Rev. Robert Hole, Fellow of
Trinity, and Beverley, went to Burwell. The Vice-
Chancellor preached. After the service they proceeded to the Manor House, where the usual
substantial dinner, and the same excellent ale and
port (which I have before described), were most
liberally served.

The Clerk, at the accustomed time, announced
that the bells were ringing—he was succeeded by
the Sexton; all but the Vicar seemed deaf to the

announcement. He had for the last three years preached an afternoon sermon, out of compliment to the Vice-Chancellor.

Although he did not consider it befitting him to remind the Vice-Chancellor that the time for departure had arrived, he fully imagined he should be very soon overtaken, as the carriage had for some time been waiting to convey the party to church.

After the Vicar's departure, the host observed, that a sermon in the afternoon at their church was quite unusual. The Vice-Chancellor asked, "What sort of a preacher is Mr Turner?" to which the tenant replied, "For my own part, I would not go over the threshold to hear him preach". "If that be your opinion, who have had frequent opportunities of hearing him," said Dr Gretton, "I am of your opinion too; and we will remain and have a few more glasses of your fine old port." The horses were then taken from the carriage, and the Vicar, after waiting a considerable time for the Vice-Chancellor before he began the service, was at length obliged to proceed without him. His indignation at such uncourteous treatment was very great, and he complained on every occasion of the insult he had received from the Vice-Chancellor.

The time for leaving was not a welcome announcement. After they commenced their homeward journey, they were in high glee, and unanimous in the praise of the tenant's substantial dinner and

the excellence of the ale and wine, which had been
so cordially pressed upon them. At length Hole
began to joke on Beverley. Now Beverley was *at
times* easily provoked; occasionally, you might say
of him whatever you pleased—he was perfectly
callous, and the most cutting sarcasms made no
impression upon him; but then he had a good deal
of wit, and was not restrained by any considera-
tions of propriety or decorum from indulging it at
the expense of any one who had offended him; besides this, Hole was a most vulnerable character,
and had forgotten that excellent adage, that "a
man who has glass windows should not throw
stones". Beverley made a furious attack upon
him, and Hole smarted severely under it. The
Vice-Chancellor came to the rescue; and Beverley
treated him with scarcely more ceremony than he
observed towards his friend. Just before they left
Newmarket Heath, the Vice-Chancellor stopped
the carriage, and ordering the Marshal to open the
door, observed that Mr Beverley's conduct was so
gross he would no longer travel in the same carriage
with him, and suggested an exchange of places with
the Marshal. Beverley answered, that he had the
same right to an inside place as the Vice-Chancellor;
that, as a Master of Arts, he had paid *as much* towards the conveyance as a Doctor of Divinity; and
that, if the Vice-Chancellor and his friend did not
like to travel with him, he recommended them to

get out of the carriage, and find their way to New-market. *They declined following his advice,* and the journey was resumed. It was not long before perfect quiet reigned amongst them, and the Marshal imagined (and it was not a *very improbable* conclusion) that the trio had been overtaken by the *drowsy god.*

The convening before the Heads, with which Beverley had been threatened during the fray, *never took place.*

University Addresses

Addresses were voted during this month by the University and Corporation, congratulating the King on the successful termination of the battle of the Nile. On the morning following the presentation, I called on a merchant in the city, who had taken his degree at the sister University. He told me that after their address had been presented, he remained with his friend Canning, to see the presentation of ours, and that they had a hearty laugh at our expense.

Vol. II, *pp.* 98–99. November 1798

It unfortunately happened that several of our deputation were not particularly well calculated to make a good figure in a procession. The Vice-Chancellor was a martyr to the gout, and so extremely deaf, that he never knew whether he was speaking in a high or low tone. Dr Douglas had but one eye, and was a perfect skeleton. The

Registrary (George Borlase) was afflicted with black
jaundice; and Broderip, of King's, was just re-
covering from yellow jaundice. Another of the
deputation was a cripple, but I cannot just now
remember his name.

One of Canning's observations was—"What have
we here? If Pope Gregory had seen this assemblage, he would not have said, '*Haud Angli, sed
Angeli*'; his observation would more probably have
been, '*Neque Angeli! neque Angli!*'"

The justice of this remark will not be questioned,
if perchance it falls under the observation of any
one who should happen to remember those who
formed at least one-half of the deputation.

At the presentation of a University address,
Beverley (as Senior Esquire Bedell) announced (as
they were presented) the names of those persons
who were to kiss hands. On one occasion he
usurped the office of the Lord in Waiting, and presented an undergraduate as about to take leave,
previous to proceeding to Russia. This unwarrant-
able liberty was strongly censured.

Vol. II,
*pp.*201–
209.
1806

In the month of January, an Address from the
University, congratulating the King on the success
of the naval victories of Lord Nelson and Sir
Richard Strachan, and lamenting the death of the
former, was presented by Dr Turner, Vice-Chancellor, attended by a deputation from the Senate,

and accompanied by the Archbishop of Canterbury, the Duke of Rutland, and many other distinguished members of the nobility.

Upon this occasion the Vice-Chancellor and deputation occupied apartments at Gray's Inn Coffee House in Holborn, where on the day of our arrival we dined. Soon after dinner, a note was put into the Vice-Chancellor's hands, who, laughing as he perused it, gave it me to read aloud. The contents produced much amusement, at the expense of the Junior Proctor, whose morality was strongly impugned. The Proctor seemed to be at first dumb with amazement, of which his countenance was a true index. He then assured the Vice-Chancellor that he had never even heard the name of the lady; and though he was born in London, he left it when five weeks old, and had never visited the great city until that very afternoon.

I rose very early to take my departure, and apologised to the Vice-Chancellor for leaving him; stating that as I so seldom visited town, I could not forego seeing the celebrated pantomime of "Mother Goose", which was at that time attracting large audiences. The Proctor expressed a wish to accompany me, and begged me to wait a few minutes till he had dressed himself. When he returned, I was horrified at his appearance, as, over the usual evening dress of a clergyman, he had put on a pair of the coarsest *overalls*, faced with very ordinary leather, and reaching from his ankles nearly to his chin. In this costume I had to conduct him through the lobby, having previously cautioned him that the females he would see there *were not within his jurisdiction.*

It is difficult to convey, to a person who has only seen the lobby within the last twenty or thirty years, an idea of what it then was. The females, who were very numerous, were not of the most respectable character; but the gentlemen were of various descriptions, consisting of men of the Universities, members of both Houses, and persons in the highest ranks of life. To induce such men to frequent the theatres, the managers gave free tickets of admission to all ladies who applied, provided they were handsome, and not likely to create a disturbance. They were admitted to every part of the house, except the dress-circles. Our entrance created a sensation; for, unluckily, many of the undergraduates (who had come up to town at that time) were present, and the exclamation, "Here's the Proctor!" was uttered by a number of voices. I passed through as quickly as I could, and desired the box-keeper to procure us seats without delay. He assured me there was not a single place vacant, except in the upper tier. I hastened there, and was conducted to a box over the stage-box, where I was told we should find room. The front seat, which would hold three, was only occupied by two well-dressed ladies. I told them that my friend was quite a stranger in London, and they *very courteously* made way for him to sit between them. I sat behind; but as some of his Cambridge friends had found out where the Proctor was situated, and were constantly opening the door, I was obliged to look for another seat, and saw no more of him that evening.

The following morning we breakfasted with the Vice-Chancellor, who told us that Lord Althorp had been there to canvass, Sir Walter Farquhar having declared that Mr Pitt could not live through the night. I learned very soon after that an express arrived from Fulham before day-break at the Speaker's, informing him of the death of that distinguished man.

We presented our Address at St James's, at two o'clock on that day. I was surprised to find that the persons whom we usually met there greeted us with the same smiling countenances they had usually worn. Lord Liverpool looked rather gloomy; but it was impossible to conjecture, from the appearance of the other Ministers, that anything had befallen their illustrious leader. An active canvass commenced at the Thatched-house Tavern, where we assembled; and Lord Henry Petty, who was likely to form one of a new Administration (if it should take place), was highly satisfied with the commencement of his canvass.

The Proctor, on his return, not being able to find his hat, and remembering he had left it in the coffee-room the previous evening, inquired very civilly of the waiter if he knew where it was. He answered in the negative, and impertinently asked if *he was sure* he brought it home; to which the Proctor answered that he was *quite sure*, having walked home.

Supposing he was not likely to have any occasion for a hat till he took a college-living, he was unwilling to buy one; and I, happening to have a spare hat, prevailed on him to use it during the remainder of his stay in town.

The same waiter who had taken advantage of the Proctor's inexperience to deprive him of his hat, acted very differently towards Mr Beverley. That very same morning he applied to him in a very loud and authoritative tone, exclaiming, "What the devil have you done with my umbrella, which I left in the coffee-room last evening?" The waiter replied very submissively, that he would go and seek it. He shortly returned with about a dozen in his hands, out of which Beverley, selecting the best, told him that he was a very impudent fellow for taking away *his property*; and if he ever served him so again, he would apply to his master to discharge him.

On the morning after the presentation of the Address, I met Beverley in Cockspur-street, who asked me if I should like to see Carlton House? I said I certainly should, but I imagined it was not to be seen by strangers. He replied, "I have a friend there who has authorized me to bring any person who may wish to see it". We were then entering Pall Mall; and when we reached Carlton House, he gave a thundering rap at the door, which was opened by the gigantic porter. "Is Mr Cole within?" said Beverley. "No, Sir," said the porter, rather gruffly.

I rejoiced to hear him say so, as I had already repented of an introduction under such auspices. Beverley, however, was not to be so repulsed; but, taking me by the arm, conducted me to a side entrance, where he rang the bell, and the door was opened by a Swiss. "Is Mr Cole within?" repeated Beverley. The Swiss, in broken English, answered "No; he is out for the day". "It is devilishly un-lucky," said Beverley, "as he desired me to bring my friend to see the house."

"If Mr Cole were within, he could not", said the Swiss, "show it you, as his Royal Highness ex-pects company to breakfast with him." Beverley, however, still urged me forward, till we arrived at the great hall, where he directed my attention to the grand staircase as worthy of notice: the Swiss followed us, and wished us to retire. Beverley was determined to proceed to that part of the house which the Prince himself inhabited. I said, "I will

not stir another step; we shall meet the Prince".
"The very thing I wish," said Beverley; "for I
have a favour to ask of him, and which I have little
doubt of his granting, for we frequently meet at
Hinchinbrooke." I expressed my determination to
return.

As we re-crossed the court-yard, I saw a member
of Parliament (whom I knew by sight) go up the
front steps. As he was *in opposition*, he had been
summoned to meet the party, to consider the line
of conduct they should adopt in consequence of
Pitt's death. As the colossal porter opened the gate
for us, Beverley said to him, "Who is the gentleman you have just let in?" "I don't know,"
surlily answered the porter. Beverley replied,
"Why, he is a member of Parliament; you must
know him". "No, I don't," said the man; and
added, "If I did" (as he was shutting the door
with great violence), "*I should not tell you.*"

It was a great relief to me to hear the gate closed
behind us, and to find myself again in Pall Mall.

When, at a subsequent period, Lord Palmerston
represented the University, he frequently invited
the deputation and some of his personal friends to
dine with him at his house in Stanhope-street. His
dinners were excellent, and his wines in great
variety, and of first-rate quality.

Returning from one of these liberal entertainments, those who had not a carriage agreed on walking together. I must acknowledge our party was very noisy; but as we *kept moving*, we arrived at the Haymarket without interruption. We reached the Opera House soon after eleven o'clock, where *our leaders* stopped to read the announcement of a new ballet, which they determined to see. Two of the number who entered were (I well remember) Sir Isaac Pennington and Professor Christian, who, with cocked hats on their heads, and red handkerchiefs on their throats to defend them from the evening air, loudly called upon the whole party to follow them. I did not accept the invitation, and therefore did not know what became of them. The *omnibus* was not then invented; they must therefore have made their way through Fops' Alley, where doubtless their costume and manner attracted general observation.

In the month of April of this year, an Address was presented at Carlton House by Dr Kaye, Vice-Chancellor, congratulating the Prince Regent on the re-establishment of peace. *Vol. II, pp. 276–277. 1816*

After the Address, we dined at the hotel in the Adelphi, where a very curious scene presented itself. Beverley was displaying, after dinner, what he called a most valuable agate snuff-box, which was handed round the table for inspection. Shortly afterwards Beverley missed this snuff-box, and said, in a very loud tone, that some one of the company had *pocketed* it. As he pronounced these words, he looked very steadfastly towards Dr Clarke (the Professor of Mineralogy), saying, "I saw it last in your hands!" The Doctor was seated next the Vice-Chancellor, and indignantly disclaimed any knowledge of it, and, jumping up, turned all his pockets inside out, proposing that the whole of the company should do the same. The Vice-Chancellor differed from him in opinion, and suggested that Beverley should quit the party, of whom he had formed so unfavourable an opinion. Beverley then left the room; but came back, and re-opening the door, said to Dr Clarke in a very loud tone, "Remember, Sir, that box is agate!" to which Clarke replied, with great animation, "Italian jasper, by the living God!" Beverley afterwards found the snuff-box about his own person.

TRINITY COLLEGE

*Vol. II, pp.*100–104   Whoever will attend to the election of Fellows, which took place from the time when Dr Postlethwaite became Master in 1789, to 1798 (which Milner speaks of as the period during which men were elected from a regard to Jacobinical and heterodox principles), will see that the insinuation is false and groundless.

Perhaps in no period, since the foundation of the

Society, have a greater number of eminent men been elected. That disgraceful system by which the actual Seniors[1] in several instances elected the Fellows, though they were not present during the Examination, and had not tested the Exercises, was abolished. Every friend to that illustrious Society will reverence the memory of John Baynes, Miles Popple, George Waddington, Thomas Cautley, Thomas Jones, Henry Porter, Kingsman Basket, John Hailstone, Matthew Murfitt, and Matthew Wilson, by whose courage and integrity that infamous practice was abolished.

The above Fellows presented a memorial to the Master and Seniors, remonstrating against a custom which was in opposition to the college statutes, and tended to destroy the objects of the foundation. The Master and Seniors, after an ineffectual attempt to induce some of the memorialists to withdraw their names, pronounced an admonition, cautioning them to behave with more deference to their superiors. From this sentence John Baynes and Miles Popple appealed to the Visitor.

On the 3rd of November, 1787, this appeal was heard in Lincoln's Inn Hall before Lord Thurlow (Lord High Chancellor of Great Britain), acting on behalf of the King, who was the real Visitor. The Lord Chancellor said, "That the practice of the electors of Fellows not examining the candidates

[1] This is possibly a slip for "the eight Seniors".

previous to election, which was complained of in
the memorial, for presenting which, the sentence
now appealed from was pronounced, was a practice
highly improper; and that the electors, even if they
were not positively required by the statutes of the
college to examine the candidates, would be bound
to do it". At the same time, he said that he did
"not approve of the manner in which the Junior
Fellows had endeavoured to reform this practice,
by presenting a memorial, like a remonstrance, to
the Seniors: that they ought to have exhibited a
charge before the Master and Seniors, against that
Senior Fellow who had elected without having examined, and should have proceeded criminally
against him: that the Master and Senior Fellows
had no means of reforming the abuse but by such
a criminal proceeding; for no recommendation or
resolution of theirs would add to the positive in-
junctions contained in the statutes: that respect to
the Seniors ought to be preserved in the college:
that it was much to be wished that the matter
should be settled without his making any decision:
that it was the interest of the whole college that
the sentence should not stand on record in the
college against the gentlemen who had signed the
memorial, and who were rising to the highest situ-
ations in the college". His Lordship added, that
"he thought the Junior Fellows ought to acknowledge that they were sensible that the manner in

which they had expressed their intention had gone further than they designed, and that the Master and Senior Fellows should expunge the censure from the Conclusion Book; and he recommended it to the parties to let the appeal stand over, in order to see whether, in the meantime, some accommodation of this kind could not be come to between them ". This being agreed to, the further consideration of the appeal was adjourned.

The Chancellor heard no more of the appeal. The offensive monition was withdrawn, and from that time to the present the Fellows have been elected with the utmost impartiality, and solely with reference to their qualifications.

From the date of this memorable appeal, Trinity College assumed that high character in the University which it has ever since maintained. The system of favouritism which had so long prevailed, and by the operation of which so many unfit men had been elected into fellowships, received its death-blow.

From 1787 to the present period, I have never heard an unsuccessful candidate hint a suspicion that he had been unfairly dealt with, and, from the paucity of vacancies, there must be many such every year.

The Master at the time of the appeal was Dr Hinchliffe, Bishop of Peterborough. That "*detur*

digniori" was not always the maxim which in-
fluenced him in disposing of a place, was apparent
from the well-known fact that he had (when a
vacancy occurred in their choir) decided in favour
of a person with an indifferent voice, *because he had
a vote* in Northamptonshire.

In some lines attributed to Mansel, this circumstance is thus alluded to:—

> A singing man and yet not sing!
> Come, justify your patron's bounty;
> Give us a song—Excuse me, Sir,
> My voice is in another county!

The Rev. Moore Meredith, B.D. was at this time
Vice-Master of the Society. He preserved that
character for wit and fancy by which he had been
so much distinguished in early life, having also
lived very much with the most celebrated wits of
the age. In some beautiful verses distributed at
his funeral (written by Henry Soame, an undergraduate of great promise), he was truly described
as one "whom Yorick honoured, and Eugenius
loved!"

Returning with my father from Ely, in August
1784, we met Mansel near Denny Abbey (accompanied by his faithful dog *Isaac*), taking his usual
walk. He asked my father to dine in the hall, and
to bring me with him. My father doubted whether
I could dine there with propriety, as I had been
admitted at Christ's College; but Mansel decided

that as I had never put on my gown, I ought not to be considered as a member of the University.

It is a curious thing that dining in that hall, in August 1849, with my friend Sedgwick, a question arose whether an undergraduate could dine at the Fellows' table, and I mentioned my having done so, as a case in point.

I well remember the day I dined there. Meredith was in great spirits; and, from our first assembling round *the Charcoal* to our quitting it after dinner, he kept the company in a roar of laughter.

I will proceed by enumerating the Seniority of Trinity College at the time of the Appeal.

Vol. II, *pp.* 106– 114

Having previously mentioned Meredith as Vice-Master, the next in order was the Rev. Stephen Whisson, B.D. He was Sub-Librarian of the University, and was, I believe, a very respectable man.

The Rev. James Backhouse, B.D., like most of the Seniority, was considered a man of gallantry; but Cambridge not being the scene of his *amours*, he was not thought so immoral as the rest. I think he had the living of Shudy Camps, in this county, but he lived a good deal at Balsham, where he was supposed to have formed a connexion not of the most reputable kind. He instituted a school for females, in the management of which he was much censured. Porson, who had described the failings

of the Seniority in some powerful satirical verses,
alluded to this circumstance in the following lines
—the only lines in the whole poem I can venture to
quote:

> Was it profit that he sought?
> No; he paid them to be taught.
> Had he honour for his aim?
> No; he *blush'd to find it fame!*

Perhaps the most singular character amongst
them all was the Rev. Samuel Peck, B.D. He had
a good deal of antiquarian knowledge, and knew
more of *village* law than the chairman of the
Quarter Sessions. At that time there were very
few magistrates in this county, and not one clergyman in the Commission of the Peace. Peck knew
the times when the overseers of the poor and the
surveyors of highways ought to be appointed, and
their various duties. I have heard several of the
Judges relate instances of the adroitness with
which (when they met at Trinity Lodge) he contrived to extract from them their opinions on
questions arising out of the 43rd cap. of Elizabeth,
and which had not been finally decided.

An opinion once prevailed in this county (and
I fear in many others), that when a person had
been bitten by a mad dog, and symptoms of having
taken the infection showed themselves, the relations of the suffering party were justified in
smothering the patient between two feather-beds.
This question he formally proposed to the Judges,

and to their answer, that "persons thus acting would undoubtedly be guilty of murder", he gave all possible publicity. For this he deserved great credit, as I have heard persons of undoubted veracity declare that it was considered not only to be legal, but really to be an act of kindness.

Those who had offended against the regulations of the Excise or Customs were in the habit of applying to Peck to memorialize the Commissioners or the Lords of the Treasury; and I am persuaded that no attorney in the town would draw up documents better than he did.

His rooms were over the Queen's Gateway; and on a Saturday, from 8 A.M. till 4 or 5 P.M., country people were constantly going to and from his rooms. To his clients he used to say, "A lawyer would have put you to expense: Sam Peck never takes a fee, but he loves gratitude; and he will accept a few sausages, a joint of pork, a couple of fowls, a goose or a turkey, or *any article* that your farm produces".

In the evening his boy came from Grantchester with a light cart, to fetch away the provisions that had been brought in the course of the day.

Whoever wishes to have a perfect idea of this extraordinary man will see in the Buttery of Trinity a likeness of him, by Bareblock, of King's. Himself, his horse, his servant, and his dog, are delineated with most astonishing accuracy.

I cannot better finish my history of Peck than by relating Dr Seale's account of his journey with him from town, in the coach so well known by the name of the *Fly*.

When Seale arrived at Gray's Inn Lane, he found Peck and two ladies already seated, who appeared to be entire strangers to each other. At Epping Place the passengers stopped to breakfast, when Peck suggested that the ladies ought not to be allowed to pay any share, which Seale immediately agreed to. The coach then proceeded to Chesterford, where the expense of dinner was shared by the gentlemen, the ladies signifying by their approving smiles that they had a due sense of the liberality of their companions. On arriving at Trumpington, the coachman pulled up, and Peck's man was in waiting to convey *the party* to Grantchester. These *ladies were, in fact,* Peck's housekeeper and housemaid, who had for some years lived with him in a very equivocal capacity.

The next in succession was the Rev. Thomas Wilson, B.D., who held the office of Bursar. He was universally known by the name of "Parabōla", from having so pronounced that word when he was keeping an Act in the schools. He lived in the rooms at present occupied by Mr Romilly, to which a garden is attached, and he had a huge padlock placed on the outside of his garden-gate.

The following reason was assigned for locking him in: As he was standing at the gate one night, Mrs Hinchliffe was returning to the Lodge, attended by her servant with a glass lantern. The latter had stepped forward to ring the bell, and her mistress was accosted by the Bursar (who mistook her for a lady who had promised to visit him), and invited to his rooms.

The Bursar, discovering his mistake, retreated hastily through the garden to his own apartment.

Mr Cranke, the Tutor (who was a particular friend of my father), used to relate these circumstances to justify himself, as the opposite garden belonged to him, and a similar padlock was placed on *his* gate to exclude all dogs from the college. This circumstance particularly annoyed Mansel, as it obliged him to carry his favourite "Isaac" in his arms through both courts when he took his walk.

A young man of Trinity, named Tom Carter, was patronised by "Parabōla", and we used to call him the "Paraboloid". He had been a pupil of Dawson's at Sedburgh, and came to college with the reputation of being a great mathematician: he failed in the schools, and took an Ægrotat degree. He was, however, appointed Mathematical Tutor to Prince William, and continued in that capacity till his Royal Highness took his degree, soon after which, Carter was made Dean of Tuam, and kept that preferment till August 1849, when he died of the cholera.

Of the Rev. John Higgs, B.D., and the Rev. Thomas Spencer, B.D., I remember but little. Spencer had been Curate of St Mary's, and during that time was guilty of great eccentricities in the reading-desk. One day, after giving out the chapter appointed for the first lesson, he added, "A very good and a very long chapter; much too good and too long for you. I'll give each of you a verse", addressing half-a-dozen elderly females who formed his daily congregation: for at that time prayers were read every morning at Great St Mary's.

His malady, which had been long suspected, was now evident, and he was removed from college. He partially recovered, and with Higgs used to come into residence whenever the Master required their votes.

Of the Rev. William Collier, B.D. (universally called "Bob Collier"), I have previously spoken[1], as having taken an emigrant Countess under his protection. He had been Tutor of the college, and was for nearly twenty years Professor of Hebrew; he was an admirable classic, and particularly well versed in modern languages (at that time a very rare accomplishment in the University). Collier

[1] See Gunning's *Reminiscences* (2nd Edition), Vol. i, p. 247: not included in these selections.

led a most dissolute life; he was also a notorious
gourmand.

An anecdote I had from his own mouth will
prove his title to the latter character. "When I
was last in town", said he, "I was going to dine
with a friend, and passed through a small court,
just as a lad was hanging up a board, on which was
this tempting inscription:

'*A roast pig this instant set upon the table!*'

"The invitation was irresistible—I ordered a
quarter; it was *very delicate* and *very delicious.* I
despatched a second and a third portion, but was
constrained to leave one quarter behind, as my
dinner hour was approaching, and my friend was
remarkably punctual."

His appearance was precisely that of a friar (as
caricatured on the English stage). I remember
being present at Stourbridge theatre, when the
Spanish Friar was performed. On the entrance of
the Friar, all eyes turned from the stage to the
side-box where the Professor was sitting; for so
perfect was the resemblance that many persons
expected to find his seat vacant.

The Rev. James Lambert was tenth Wrangler
and senior medallist in 1764. He was two years
junior to Collier, and had been for nine years Greek
Professor. His health was very indifferent; he
therefore resided a good deal at Abingdon with the

Rev. Andrew Perne, formerly of Peterhouse. Botany was his favourite pursuit, in addition to which he was passionately fond of fishing and shooting; he made his own tackle, and was one of the most skilful fly-fishers I ever met with. Lambert was supposed not to be quite orthodox, for which suspicion I am not aware there was any other foundation than that he appeared with Jones and Tyrwhitt as the supporters of Frend, against what they considered a malicious prosecution for political opinions, under pretext of a regard for the Established Religion. Lambert was never addicted to those vices for which at that time the Seniors of Trinity were so notorious; but, when in college, attended closely to literary pursuits. He was made Bursar by Dr Postlethwaite, and during the time he held the situation, was considered a very active and judicious officer.

Lightning Source UK Ltd.
Milton Keynes UK
UKOW04f0944101115

262431UK00001B/11/P